Island Thyme

TASTES AND TRADITIONS OF BERMUDA

Dedication

To all the people, especially women,

who volunteer their time to charities

in Bermuda—this book is for you.

The BJSL wants to recognise

your efforts and reward them.

The proceeds of this cookbook

will be donated to different local

organisations and individuals,

to aid your efforts in helping

our community.

Island Thyme

TASTES AND TRADITIONS OF BERMUDA

THE BERMUDA JUNIOR SERVICE LEAGUE

Island Thyme

TASTES AND TRADITIONS OF BERMUDA

Published by The Bermuda Junior Service League

Registered Bermuda Charity #106

ISBN: 1-894916-28-X

Edited, Designed, and Manufactured by Favorite Recipes® Press

an imprint of

FRP

P.O. Box 305142, Nashville, Tennessee, USA 37230

800-358-0560

Art Director: Steve Newman

Book Design: David Malone

Project Manager: Ashley Bienvenu

Project Editor: Jane Hinshaw

Manufactured in the United States of America

First Printing 2005

20,000 copies

Preface

At the time this book launches, The Bermuda Junior Service League (BJSL) will be celebrating the thirtieth anniversary of our original cookbook, *Bermudian Cookery*. After thirty years, *Bermudian Cookery* has sold over a quarter of a million copies and has been a major fundraiser for the BJSL. To pay tribute to the success of the original cookbook and to provide additional funds to support the BJSL's mandate, *Island Thyme* has been developed.

The herb Thyme, grows extensively in Bermuda's kitchen gardens and is used in a number of the recipes in this book. Bermudians pride themselves on their friendly nature and relaxed pace referred to as being on "Island time." Hence the play on words in the title of this cookbook.

With a committee of twelve women and the support of the entire BJSL and many businesses and friends, it has taken just under two years to develop. Hours of fun, brainstorming, eating, and photo shoots have come together to show the pride we feel about our organisation and Bermuda. We hope that this cookbook provides you with many useful recipes and a further appreciation of the tastes and traditions of our Island, Bermuda.

Thank you to our spouses, families, and friends who supported us for nearly two years. To those of you who babysat, shopped, cooked, tasted, tended bar, and parked cars, our heartfelt thanks! We couldn't have done it without you.

COOKBOOK COMMITTEE

Dawn Dunstan
Louise Gibbons
Deborah Titterton Narraway
Elizabeth Lindgren
Mollie Myer
Kimberly Paterson
Wendi Ryland
Susan Smith
Tegan Smith
Diane Steiger
Carolyn Toogood
Elizabeth Zalinger

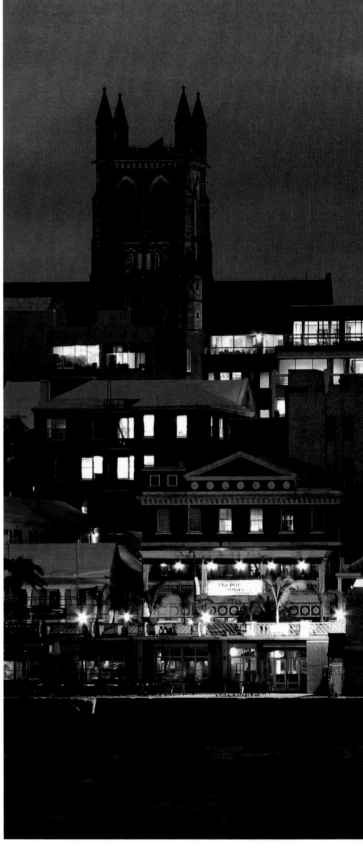

TRADITIONS OF *Bermuda*

A NIGHT OUT IN *Bermuda*

TASTES OF *Bermuda*

Contents

Foreword

The Bermuda Junior Service League (BJSL) is an organisation of women committed to promoting volunteerism, developing the potential of women, and improving the community in which we live. Its purpose is educational and charitable.

Reading Lefroy's *Memorials of the Bermudas*, one is struck by the constant references to the Island's abundant wildlife. For thousands of years Bermuda basked in the mid-Atlantic sunshine, its atolls rising up from the deepest ocean to create a perfect environment for fish and molluscs. Larger predators could swim up from the ocean floor and feed, whales dropped by for plankton, and migrating birds sought rest and relaxation in the lush greenery. Into this land of plenty arrived the settlers, most escaping famine, poverty, and political or religious intolerance. What they found must have seemed like heaven on earth. With the exception of natural springs, Bermuda offered everything, and in a few short years its early inhabitants were on their way to building a community.

Early settlers built Bermuda cottages, small two- or three-roomed affairs made from hand-cut limestone quarried nearby, with Bermuda cedar floors, window frames, and beams. A fireplace with a tripod for pots and perhaps a small side brick oven for baking was central to the main room. Cedar furniture and utensils were commonplace, while iron frying pans and pots made up the family's kitchenware. Chickens, goats, pigs, turkeys, and the occasional cow could be found alongside kitchen gardens that yielded greens, sweet potatoes, vegetables, and herbs. In the coastal areas, fishing nets would be hung from cedar trees, and the air was heavy with the buzz of cicadas.

Local communities tended to forge strong links and, in Bermuda, sharing became a way of life. A neighbour with a large oven would bake once a week in exchange for some eggs or a piece of pork. Another might "rake" salt (in Bermuda, seawater was evaporated in shallow pans) and exchange this precious commodity for salt fish or mullet. Beef was not a staple, although it was occasionally available from various markets. Salt beef was imported from England, as were many staples like flour, sugar, and butter, while the triangle trade routes (Bermuda, the Caribbean, and Eastern Canada) provided salt cod, rum, molasses, and salt. Today Bermuda's cuisine can trace its roots, as can most Caribbean islands, to the trade routes. Salt cod became a staple, molasses was the islander's sweetener, and rum his anaesthetic.

Cassava root, introduced from the Caribbean, worked its way into our national dish. Though used extensively throughout the Caribbean and Central America for bread or cake, grated cassava made into the rich, meaty pie of Bermuda is unique. Associated with Christmas celebrations, it was both expensive and time-consuming to prepare: grating and squeezing; collecting dozens of eggs; using refined sugar, grated nutmeg, chicken, and pork. Families who could afford to make cassava pies established a tradition of giving pies over the holidays.

It is the day-to-day diet that helps to build a community's identity, and Bermudians ate seafood. Turtles were popular and abundant, hundred-pound groupers were speared around the rocks, and mullets were netted by the thousands to be hung out under a hot sun to dry. Industrious fishermen salted large bream, using it as Bermudians today use salt cod. Seafood stews were popular, often enlivened with mussels, oysters, or conch obtained either by diving or from the mussel men of Bailey's Bay and Harrington Sound. Suck rock, made from prising trilobites from along the rocky shores and simmering them for hours with pawpaw, took a lot of work for mixed results, while shark hash, another of Bermuda's most intriguing dishes, is still in demand. Shark hash is a traditional dish unique to Bermuda. Flaky and lightly spiced with peppers, baby pumpkin leaves, and chopped parsley, it is a culinary marvel that lords over more contemporary delights such as mussel pie or conch stew.

No social history would be complete without mention of chutneys, jams, and jellies, which added variety and sweetness to every table. Pawpaw (papaya) and loquat were made into sweet pies, chutneys, and jams. Surinam cherry, bay grape, citrus, and cactus plum were made into jams and jellies for Sunday or for after-school treats, while banana, sweet potato, coconut, and cassava found themselves in breads and puddings. From gingerroot, lemon grass, and palmetto berry came cool drinks. Teas were brewed from dried leaves, bark, or grasses collected from backyard gardens or the open countryside and used for any manner of ailment.

As a strong part of this community, the BJSL has been contributing towards our health and well-being since 1936. Members are required to give a minimum of fifty service hours each year to help raise funds and implement and manage the success of their many programmes. From its close working relationship with Keep Bermuda Beautiful to its ongoing support of the local hospital, BJSL members do make a difference.

I remember the League through its original cookbook, perhaps the most successful such book published in Bermuda. My present copy dates from 1983 and is well thumbed and still useful. Much of the fun is reading through it and trying to imagine the ladies, many familiar to me, making these dishes—or not, as I suspect the case to be at times! The cookbook does, however, serve an excellent purpose and that is to bring together recipes from our community to share with others, for the benefit of all.

I would like to thank the membership for inviting me to write this foreword, for what is sure to be an excellent and highly prized addition to Bermuda's culinary—and publishing—scene. I extend my best wishes to them for its success and for their success in the coming years.

Joe Gibbons

TRADITIONS OF

Bermuda

The Easter Season

GOOD FRIDAY is a fantastic family celebration. There is nothing more beautiful than a sky filled with colourful

Bermudian paper kites on Good Friday. After church, families and friends gather at beaches such as Horseshoe

Bay and at family homes for kite-flying and a picnic lunch of codfish cakes and hot cross buns. Open spaces

soon fill up with kite-flyers and picnickers.

THE PASSION FLOWER

There is a traditional Easter legend surrounding the Passion flower. The Passion flower grows on a climbing vine and has ten identical petals said to represent the disciples, excluding Peter and Judas. The double rows of coloured filaments appear to show the halo around the head of Christ or the crown of thorns. The violet stamens show the wounds and nails of Christ's crucifixion.

BERMUDA PAPER KITES

The simplest Bermudian paper kites are made using heavy brown paper and a frame in the shape of a cross. This religious tradition is believed to have been started by a Sunday school teacher teaching about the Ascension of Christ. The teacher built a kite out of two sticks in the shape of a cross, covered the sticks with an image of Christ, and launched the kite into the air. Once flying, the kite was cut free, and the children were able to watch the kite float up and away. Today's Bermudian kites are usually made of wooden sticks up to six feet in length, coloured tissue paper, string, and the cloth of old bed sheets. Pieces of tissue paper are added to the head of the kite to vibrate in the breeze, causing a distinct humming sound.

Good Friday Menu

Codfish Cakes

Rice Salad

Coleslaw

Baked Beans

Hot Cross Buns

Banana Bread

Carrot Cake with
Cream Cheese Frosting

Mint Sun Tea

HOT CROSS BUNS AND CODFISH CAKES

Bermudians have created their own traditional Easter delicacy by placing a codfish cake in a hot cross bun. Hot cross buns are said to have originated with the Anglo-Saxons, who ate the sacramental cakes in honour of the goddess Eastore. British-style hot cross buns have a white icing cross applied to the top to signify Christ's suffering on the cross. Bermudian hot cross buns may have either a white icing cross or a cross cut into the top of each bun before baking.

EASTER SUNDAY in Bermuda starts at sunrise when nondenominational services are held outdoors at places like Horseshoe Bay Beach and Elbow Beach. After church, families often return home to have a large traditional codfish and potato breakfast. Easter dinner is often a family affair with a large ham being served.

Like most children, Bermudian children awake Easter morning with the hope that the Easter bunny has visited their home. Often parents will hide the Easter eggs and treats around the house or in the garden for the children to find.

EASTER LILY

The lily is a symbol of purity because of its whiteness and delicacy of form. It also symbolises innocence and the radiance of the Lord's risen life. It is called the Easter lily because the flowers bloom in early spring around Easter time. A local tradition is the selection of Easter lilies to be sent to Her Majesty Queen Elizabeth II every Easter.

Easter Sunday Menu

Bermuda Codfish and Potato Breakfast

Tomato Sauce

Egg Sauce

Hot Cross Buns

Champagne

Orange Juice

The Bermuda or white trumpet lily was not originally from Bermuda; it was first introduced to the Island quite by accident in the 1850s by a disabled ship that was loaded with lilies and bulbs. The precious cargo remained on the island, never reaching its intended destination. The Bermuda Easter lily was introduced to the United States from Bermuda in the 1880s by Mrs. Thomas P. Sargent of Philadelphia. The Easter lily remains a mainstay of Easter floral arrangements and church decorations.

Bermuda Day

BERMUDA DAY, May 24, originally marked the birthday of Queen Victoria. Over time, the symbolism of

this public holiday has changed from Empire Day to Commonwealth Day and, finally, to Bermuda Day in the

1970s. It was suggested that the day be used to bring Bermudians together to celebrate their heritage and how

lucky they are to live on this tiny island paradise.

THE START OF SUMMER

Bermuda Day is considered Bermuda's first day of summer. May 24 marks the local calendar as the day Bermudians take their first swim of the year.

CELEBRATING SUMMER

Picknicking is a major activity during the summer holidays. Parks and beaches are packed with friends and families enjoying fine picnic fare. Hamilton Harbour is filled with sailboats and power boats loading up and cruising out for the day.

Bermuda Day Menu

Smoked Salmon Tortilla Rolls

Focaccia Sandwich

Shrimp Pasta Salad

Pesto Potato Salad

Devilled Eggs

Cream Cheese Brownies

Homemade Brownies

Island Fruit Salad

Pineapple Ginger Beer

THE MARATHON DERBY

The Marathon Derby, which dates back to 1909, is a half marathon run from Somerset to Hamilton. Professional and amateur runners alike are attracted by the challenge of completing this national race. Running the race, if only once, is considered a great achievement. Everyone knows at least one participant, and large crowds line the streets to encourage the athletes.

BERMUDA FITTED DINGHIES

A main event of Bermuda Day is the first Bermuda Fitted Dinghy Race of the season, held in St. George's Harbour. The racing tradition began when groups of smaller boats would ferry in the catch from the larger fishing boats. Whoever made it to the dock first sold their goods first.

The individual boats began to be fitted out with larger and larger sails in order to beat the others. Today, the 1,000 square feet of sail that the dinghies carry is more sail than any other vessel of its size. These sailing vessels are unique in design, as they are fourteen feet long with forty-foot masts and a fourteen-foot bowsprit.

THE HERITAGE DAY PARADE

The Heritage Day Parade combines flower-filled floats, marching bands, majorettes, and the Bermuda Gombeys. By late afternoon, the crowds will have gathered for refreshments, music, and all the fun of a fair at a field on the outskirts of town.

Four Bermuda Fitted Dinghies—the Elizabeth, the Challenger, the Contest, and the Victory—currently race on alternate Sundays between May 24 and mid-September. The races are a chaotic flurry of sails flapping in the wind and screaming crew members bailing out the rising water at top speed. It is not unusual to witness a dinghy actually sink below the water line. Powerboats follow the dinghies up and down the racecourse and are often called upon to collect a crewmember who has jumped overboard to lighten the load and increase the speed of the dinghy.

THE BERMUDA GOMBEY

"Gombey" is a Bantu word meaning rhythm and drum; the dance originated in Africa and came to Bermuda via the Caribbean. Bermudians took the original African dances and created their own unique dance. It illustrates the energetic and colourful celebration of Bermuda's African heritage. Gombeys perform in groups called troupes that are generally composed of male dancers and musicians from one family, who maintain and pass on traditional Gombey dance techniques.

THE GOMBEY COSTUME

The handmade costumes include a cape with colourful tassels and beads; mirrors and other shiny objects are sewn on the back. The pants are embroidered with the same colourful tassels all the way around the legs and from knee to ankle. The masks are topped with bright and glittery, tall headdresses with peacock feathers on top and two long braids. The tomahawks, bows, and arrows are likely inspired by early Native American slaves. Rimmed drums are played with sticks, indicating a military and, perhaps, a mummer influence.

Bermuda Weddings

BERMUDA WEDDINGS "take the cake" as perhaps the most spectacular of Bermudian social events.

Traditionally, Bermudians marry in their church with a reception held immediately afterwards at the home

of the bride's parents.

WEDDING ATTIRE

In the heat of the summer, it is not uncommon to see a beautiful bride dressed in a sleeveless white gown. Her groom and ushers may sport traditional Bermuda attire consisting of Bermuda shorts, knee-high socks, white shirt, and colourful tie with a navy blazer.

The traditional Bermudian reception is a standing-room-only cocktail party with hundreds of invited guests and party crashers, since Bermuda is a small island, and word of a good party travels fast! There is always an open bar stocked with Bermudian favourites such as rum swizzle, rum, and ginger beer. With the hot summer weather, weddings tend to be in the late afternoon with receptions beginning at cocktail hour and going until the wee hours. Wedding receptions may also include unusual features, such as a bagpiper leading in the newlyweds, a performance by the Gombeys, or even arrival of the couple by boat.

Reception Menu

Chicken Satay with
Peanut Dipping Sauce

Cocktail Fish Cakes with Banana

Crab and Cream Cheese Tarts

Coconut Shrimp

Conch Fritters with
Island Tartar Sauce

Melon and Mozzarella
with Prosciutto

Party Crostini

Bride's Cake

Groom's Cake

Bermuda Rum Swizzle

THE BERMUDA MOONGATE

Originally inspired by Chinese aesthetics, Bermuda's first moongate was built in 1860 by a local sea captain who drew the design of a circular ornamental wooden gateway to a garden. The moongate has now become a national symbol for Bermuda. There are limestone moongates scattered all across the island. Tradition has it that people who walk through a moongate, especially young lovers and honeymooners, are blessed with good luck. This makes the moongate a romantic element that many couples include in their wedding celebration.

WEDDING CAKES

Bermudian wedding cakes are true culinary works of art. Traditionally there are always two wedding cakes, the bride's cake and the groom's cake. The bride's cake represents the traditional roles of the wife, mother, and homemaker. This cake is usually a fruitcake, iced with marzipan and royal icing, covered in glittering silver leaf, and topped with Bermuda roses and ivy.

The groom's cake represents the wealth that he brings to the union. A single-layer pound cake, iced in royal icing, and covered with 24-carat gold leaf is usually topped with a small Bermuda cedar tree. This sapling is planted by the bride and groom at the reception or immediately afterwards at their home as a sign of their love and future together.

TRADITIONAL WEDDING TRANSPORT

Wedding parties traditionally arrive at the church and reception in Bermuda surreys, or horse-drawn carriages. A "Bermudiful" sight is a smartly-dressed carriage driver in a gleaming pith helmet steering through the streets to the church with a radiant bride and her father.

MODERN WEDDING TRANSPORT

More recently, some wedding parties have hired immaculately-detailed private vehicles of the same make and colour. On a summer Saturday, lines of wedding cars can be seen adorned with ribbons on their hoods or bonnets with their horns blaring. Honking at a wedding party in their carriages or cars is considered a Bermudian greeting of "good luck" or "hello," in spite of its being against the law!

GIFT REGISTRY

Gift registries are used extensively in Bermuda. The gifts are not wrapped and delivered to the bride. Rather, a list of purchased items is added to her account. This is a true example of Bermudian practicality.

BERMUDA AS A WEDDING DESTINATION

Bermuda is a popular wedding destination. Visitors are drawn to the Island by the lush gardens and pink beaches, which are ideal settings for picturesque ceremonies and receptions. Prior to the wedding, local wedding coordinators can assist with the details in planning a Bermuda wedding.

Cup Match

CUP MATCH is an exciting two-day Bermudian holiday when the Island "jumps up" and "comes to a standstill" at once! Shops and businesses close for the Thursday and Friday of the week before the first Monday in August, while islanders enjoy boating, camping, and the annual cricket match between St. George's Cricket Club and Somerset Cricket Club. The match is a prestigious event and is hosted alternately between the two clubs.

CAMPING

Cup Match is the high point of the summer camping season. Bermuda's parks and small islands are filled with large gatherings of campers who can be found listening to the cricket game on portable radios while enjoying traditional fare.

EMANCIPATION DAY

In 1835, an American ship carrying seventy-eight slaves was driven off course by a storm. Since Bermuda had freed its slaves in 1834, they were allowed to remain in Bermuda as free individuals.

Bermuda's Afro-Bermudian population commemorates the anniversary of freedom with various celebrations, including the annual Cup Match cricket festival. Since 1902, Cup Match has been the premier event held in celebration of Emancipation Day, a day declared by the Bermuda Government to be the Thursday of each Cup Match celebration in commemoration of the ending of slavery in Bermuda.

Cup Match Menu

Conch Chowder

Shark Hash

Curried Mussel Pie

Fried Fish Sandwich

Hoppin' John

Macaroni and Cheese

Cup Match Potato Salad

Dark 'n' Stormies

SOMERS' DAY

The Friday of Cup Match is officially Somers' Day. It celebrates Sir George Somers' arrival on the Island when his ship, the Sea Venture, ran aground near the East End in a fierce storm on July 28, 1609.

HISTORY OF CUP MATCH

The Cup Match tradition began when the game of cricket was brought to Bermuda in the 1840s by British Army soldiers. British soldiers were stationed at the Royal Naval Dockyard in Somerset and the British Garrison in St.George's. Somerset and St. George's became the homes of the Island's two most famous cricket clubs.

After a particularly competitive match in 1901, both clubs decided to take up a collection to purchase a silver cup, and in 1902 the first match was played for the cup. Today that trophy is a revered national treasure and is kept safe in a bank vault; the match is now played for a duplicate cup.

CRICKET ATTIRE

The cricketers wear traditional all-white cricket dress, which contrasts dramatically with the colourful, summer, Cup Match outfits of the spectators. Large straw hats sporting the Cup Match ribbons are a prominent feature.

THE CRICKET MATCH

For most Bermudians, the annual cricket match is a paramount experience. The pitch is surrounded by the aromas of fish sandwiches, curried mussel pies, and conch stew, sold in makeshift stalls. Bar stands sell cold beer and a famous Bermudian drink, the "Dark 'n' Stormy." Cricket fans fill the stands with team colours: red and blue for Somerset, dark and light blue for St. George's. Soca music, a mix of calypso and reggae, is played loudly as crowds gather around Crown and Anchor gambling tables.

BOATING

Bermuda is a boating paradise, for the water surrounding the reefs is warm, calm, and clear, revealing stunning shades of turquoise. Islanders out boating for the Cup Match holiday typically raft their boats together for an ultimate boating party!

CROWN AND ANCHOR

Crown and Anchor is the only legalised form of gambling in Bermuda and can only be played during the two-day Cup Match holiday. The Crown and Anchor table is painted with six symbols—the crown, anchor, heart, club, diamond, and spade, corresponding to the symbols on the dice. Players place their bets on the symbol they believe the banker will roll.

Afternoon Tea

AFTERNOON TEA is one of the loveliest traditions in Bermuda. Originally introduced in England during the early 1800s by Anna, Duchess of Bedford, the practice has grown and adapted tremendously over the past 200 years.

Afternoon Tea or "low tea" is usually taken in a sitting room where the trays are placed on low tables such as coffee tables. Afternoon tea should not be confused with "high tea," which tends to be heavier and replaces dinner.

ORIGINS OF THE TEATIME TRADITIONS

During the late 1700s and early 1800s, Anna, Duchess of Bedford, began secretly "taking tea" in the late afternoon to ward off hunger. Once discovered, she began inviting others to join her. This new social custom allowed women to socialise together in the shops and parlours, provided they were accompanied by a male escort.

In England during the mid-1800s, men began enjoying midday meals at their social clubs, leaving women unable to go to public tea houses or gardens without a male escort. As a result, women began inviting other women to their homes for tea.

Afternoon Tea Menu

English Tea Sandwiches

Greek Quiche

Cranberry Scones

Apricot and Cardamom Scones

Millionaire's Shortbread

Russian Tea Cookies

Cranberry Cookies

Date Dainties

Chocolate Mint Brownies

Traditional Fruit Cake

Tea

Afternoon Tea is generally between 3 P.M. and 5 P.M. and includes three courses served in a specific order. Savouries of tiny sandwiches or appetisers come first. They are followed by scones served with jam and clotted cream or Devonshire cream. Pastries of cookies, tarts, cakes, and shortbread are served last.

AT HOME HOURS

In the 19th Century, women began to schedule time when a lady would remain at home one day a week to receive visitors. Women sent an "At Home Hours" notice, and it was expected that, unless regrets were sent, all who received a notice would attend. Conversation was the entertainment, and tea, cakes, sandwiches, or other niceties were served.

The hostess would always pour the tea and add the sugar, milk, or lemon to the tea for the guest. Often her eldest daughter or best friend would assist with the serving. At least one person held "At Home Hours" on a given day, and social ties were established as women saw each other almost daily. This practice was a tremendously liberating social change for women.

TEA TIME IN THE 20TH CENTURY

Between the 1940s and the 1970s, most Bermudian women worked in the home, and they occasionally entertained during the day. The typical party was complete with silver service, fresh flowers, fresh whipped cream, and sandwiches presented on beautiful china.

AFTERNOON TEA AT GOVERNMENT HOUSE

These photographs were taken at an Afternoon Tea held at Government House. Tea at Government House is not a daily affair but is reserved for special occasions and important guests, such as royalty, local and overseas dignitaries, and members of government. Tea may be served to guests in the privacy of their suites of rooms or enjoyed as a group in the large formal dining room.

TEA TIME IN THE 21ST CENTURY

As women participate in the workforce in larger numbers, tea parties have become a rare luxury. Women have less time to entertain lady friends during the afternoon. However, afternoon tea can be enjoyed daily at the island's hotels, where the tea menu typically includes English tea sandwiches, pastries, and desserts.

Tea is made from the camellia plant, an evergreen with dark green, shiny leaves and small, white blossoms. Native to China, Tibet and northern India, there are two major varieties: the small leaf variety, *Camellia sinensis*, thrives in the cool, high mountain regions, and the broad leaf variety, *Camellia assamica*, grows best in tropical climates. All tea comes from the same plant, and it is the processing method that accounts for over 2,000 types of teas available today. Herbal teas or herbal infusions are not really teas but simply dried flowers and/or herbs.

The Christmas Season

THE CHRISTMAS SEASON is Bermuda's most festive social and religious holiday. Houses are decked with

bright lights, Christmas trees, wonderful foods, and celebration ensues!

CHRISTMAS EVE is the time for church, particularly family services and midnight mass. At home, the stockings are hung by the chimney and treats are left out for Santa and the reindeer. Children are usually hurried off to bed in anticipation of Santa's arrival, while the adults begin preparing for the Christmas Day feast.

During the Christmas holidays, Bermudians enjoy many fabulous festive activities. Some of the most notable include the lighting of the streetlights of St. Georges and Hamilton; the Annual Santa Claus Parade sponsored by the Bermuda Junior Chamber of Commerce; the British-style Christmas pantomime put on by The Bermuda Musical and Dramatic Society; The Royal Gazette Newspaper's annual Christmas short story contest for writers under 18 years of age; the spectacular Christmas Boat Parade in Hamilton Harbour; and the outdoor Christmas lights competition among private homes and businesses.

Treats for Santa Menu

Nutmeg Cookies

Russian Tea Cookies

Mincemeat Tarts

Traditional Fruit Cake

Bacardi Rum Cake

Espresso Chocolate Fudge

Truffles

Marble Chocolate Almond Bark

Hot Chocolate

CHRISTMAS TREES

Today, lavishly decorated Christmas trees are commonly displayed in most Bermudian homes. Spruce and other Christmas trees are imported from Canada and the United States, as they are not grown locally. To protect local flora from disease, trees are inspected by the Bermuda Government before they are sold on the island.

CHRISTMAS DAY with family and friends is one benefit to Bermudians living on an island twenty-two miles long and less than one mile wide. Christmas dinner is a wonderful opportunity for the extended family to come together and enjoy family favourites. Dinner is generally a lavish affair served using the family's best china and silver. Table settings often include British novelties called Christmas crackers. These treats are pulled open with a snap by two people. Christmas crackers are usually filled with a colourful tissue paper hat, a joke, and a small gift.

Christmas Dinner Menu

Roast Turkey

Bacon and Spinach Stuffing

Chestnut Stuffing

Gravy

Cranberry Relish

Potatoes, Carrots, and
Green Beans

Cassava Pie

Mincemeat Tarts

Christmas Pudding with
Hard Sauce and
Lemon Sauce

Wine and Port

Foods traditionally served on Christmas Day include roast turkey, baked ham, fresh stuffing, fresh vegetables, and cassava pie. Cassava pie is served as an accompaniment to roast turkey and is rightly considered a Bermudian epicurean delight. Desserts typically include rum cake and Christmas plum pudding. After dinner and dessert, guests often retire from the table to the lounge for a glass of port, which is served with a tray of grapes, Stilton cheese, and crackers.

BOXING DAY originated in Britain as a day off for all household staff following Christmas Day. Members of the merchant class would give boxes containing food and fruit, clothing, and/or money to tradespeople and servants. It is now a day of relaxing, socialising, entertaining, and finishing off the cassava pie, roast turkey, and other Christmas delights. Bermudians also enjoy annual Boxing Day outings to watch the Gombey Dancers, Motor Cross Races at Coney Island, or the Stakes Pony Races at the National Equestrian Centre track.

Boxing Day Menu

Pea Soup

Ham

Cassava Pie

Sweet White Rolls

Mincemeat Tarts

Bacardi Rum Cake

Holiday Eggnog

OPEN HOUSE ENTERTAINING

Christmas parties in Bermuda can take many forms. One of the most popular traditional events is "Open House." The host and hostess set out a buffet for guests to enjoy as they drop by during an afternoon or evening on Boxing Day, New Year's Day, or the intervening weekend.

Historic Bermuda

Government House features prominently in photographs of the Afternoon Tea and Breakfast and Brunch sections.

GOVERNMENT HOUSE stands on thirty-three acres on Langton Hill overlooking the North Shore in the Parish

of Pembroke. It was built in 1892 to replace an earlier Governor's residence called Mount Langton, named after

a Scottish estate belonging to Sir James Cockburn, Governor of Bermuda from 1814 to 1816. The architect,

William Cardy Hallet, designed the new Government House in the Italianate style which romanticised the revival

of the villas of Tuscany and Umbria characterised by square towers and asymmetrical plans.

The house consists of more than thirty rooms, including a large drawing room and a dining room for formal entertaining, both of which open onto a long enclosed glass sun terrace overlooking the pool and garden. These rooms provide the perfect space with plenty of light to display many works of art, antique furniture, and sculpture. All the paintings are of Bermudian images by artists living on the island or visiting its shores over the years. The collection continues through the corridors and upstairs in the Royal Suite, the private quarters of the Governor and his wife, and the four guest bedrooms. Some of the artwork is part of the government collection donated by individuals or by the Bermuda National Trust. The rest are on loan from the Masterworks Foundation and local artists.

Five gardeners from the Parks Department are assigned to maintain the property, which consists of a modest kitchen garden, citrus grove, banana plantation, cut flower garden, self-generating forests, meadows, and numerous small quarries planted out or covered in wild flowers, paw paws and palms. A bluebird trail of twenty nesting boxes attracts migrating and native birds year-round. Horses used to be kept in a paddock and exercised on what is now a large, open green meadow. There are three terraces with herbaceous borders and a rose garden. Many ceremonial trees have been planted by members of the Royal Family, prime ministers, presidents, cabinet ministers, governors, and first ladies. As the largest open green area in the parish of Pembroke, it has fine examples of every endemic species of vegetation, which are crucial to ward off erosion and wind damage from tropical storms, hurricanes, and winter gales. Much of the Island in the last fifty years has seen the spread of invasives which threaten the survival of these plants, and there has been a concerted effort by the current occupants of the house and the Government Parks Department to eliminate these shrubs and trees. The grounds sustained severe damage after Hurricane Fabian on September 5, 2003, and there is underway a long-term programme of clearing up, re-landscaping, and planting.

Bermuda is an Overseas Territory of the United Kingdom and enjoys a high degree of self-government. The Governor's flag is a Union Jack with the Bermuda arms on a white disk encircled by a green garland. The present Governor, Sir John Vereker, was appointed by Queen Elizabeth II. He and his wife, Lady Vereker, have resided at Government House since 2002. It has been their aim to open up Government House to all Bermudians, making the grounds and house more accessible to those who have never before visited. Professional and amateur artists have been invited to bring their palettes and brushes; apprentices in horticulture have used the grounds to do internships; Girl Guides and Boy Scouts have had plenty of room to sit around their campfires; community groups have been invited for tea and a viewing of the artwork and rooms; charities have used the formal rooms for workshops, visual presentations, lectures, meetings, and photo opportunities. This has been in addition to the traditional entertainment in the Government House social diary which is extended to those who live and work in Bermuda and those visiting from other countries.

VERDMONT is one of the most fascinating old houses in Bermuda. Verdmont's structure has remained virtually unchanged for more than 300 years. Verdmont was built in 1710 and is four-squared with four great chimneys, two at each end of the house, providing a fireplace in each of the eight rooms.

Verdmont was the ideal setting for presenting the photographs in the Soups and Salads section.

The furniture at Verdmont, made mostly of Bermuda cedar, is one of the finest collections crafted on the Island by local cabinet makers between 1700 and 1800. The portraits in the house, painted by John Green and members of his family, have hung at Verdmont since the early part of the 18th century when he took over the house. Verdmont is indeed the "Jewel in the Crown" of Bermuda's National Trust properties. No longer a private home, Verdmont is now run as a museum by the Bermuda National Trust and is open to the public.

PALM GROVE, on South Shore in Devonshire, was built in the 1800s as a working farm. It was bought from the Stone family by Edmund Gibbons in the mid-1950s. The gardens and ponds, including the well-known Map Pond, were all designed by Edmond Gibbons.

Palm Grove provided a picturesque backdrop for the photographs in the Easter Season section.

The Map Pond is a map of Bermuda, set in one of the lily ponds, built to scale and accurately oriented. The gardens feature an aviary of tropical birds, many endemic plants and trees, a beautiful moongate, and stunning South Shore views. The gardens are open to the public free of charge from Monday to Thursday, except for public holidays.

A NIGHT OUT IN

Bermuda

Built in 1727, Fourways Restaurant is one of Bermuda's treasures, exuding old world charm. Enjoy before-dinner drinks in the historical Peg Leg lounge, followed by dinner served in true gourmet style and accompanied by one of the island's finest wine selections. Fine dining and a warm welcome are provided in a relaxed and charming atmosphere.

Fourways Inn

1 Middle Road

Paget

info@fourways.bm

441-236-6517

Pan-Fried Rockfish

with Ginger and Fennel Beurre Blanc

FENNEL BEURRE BLANC

1 tablespoon chopped shallot
8 ounces fennel, sliced
6 ounces unsalted butter
8 ounces fish stock
2 ounces dry white wine
1 tablespoon Pernod (optional)
1/2 teaspoon each seasoning salt
   and pepper

PAN-FRIED ROCKFISH

4 (6-ounce) portions rockfish or
   grouper
2 teaspoons sea salt
1/2 teaspoon ground pepper
4 ounces gingerroot, finely sliced
2 ounces extra-virgin olive oil
asparagus tips
sesame oil

For the beurre blanc, sweat the shallot and fennel in 1 tablespoon of the butter in a saucepan until tender. Add the fish stock and cook until reduced by 1/2. Add the wine and cook until reduced to 1/3. Stir in the Pernod. Add the remaining butter gradually, heating until blended after each addition. Season with seasoning salt and pepper. Keep warm over low heat, taking care not to overheat to prevent the sauce from separating.

For the rockfish, rinse the portions and pat dry. Season with the sea salt and pepper and top with the gingerroot. Heat the olive oil in a nonstick skillet. Add the fish with the gingerroot side down. Pan-fry the fish until golden brown on the bottom. Turn over the fish gently and pan-fry until golden brown on the other side, for a total of 7 to 10 minutes.

To serve, spoon the beurre blanc onto serving plates. Add the fish to the plates and top with asparagus tips. Drizzle with sesame oil.

Serves 4

Chef Tommy Poh

Beef Tataki
on Vinegared Rice with Spicy Tonkatsu Dressing

SPICY TONKATSU DRESSING

1/4 cup tonkatsu sauce
1 tablespoon hot chili sauce
1 teaspoon each ketchup, sake and
   sesame oil
2 teaspoons mayonnaise

VINEGARED RICE

1 tablespoon lemon juice
4 mangos, chopped
4 avocados, chopped
salt and crushed pepper to taste
2 teaspoons rice vinegar
4 teaspoons mirin (Japanese wine)
1 teaspoon each sugar and salt
2 cups sushi rice, cooked

BEEF TATAKI

3 pounds beef strip loin
salt to taste
10 ounces crushed black
   peppercorns
4 scallions, chopped

For the dressing, combine the tonkatsu sauce, chili sauce, ketchup, sake, sesame oil and mayonnaise in a bowl and mix well.

For the rice mould with mangos and avocados, combine the lemon juice with the mangos and avocados in a bowl, tossing to coat well. Season with salt and crushed pepper to taste. Combine the rice vinegar, mirin, sugar and 1 teaspoon salt in a saucepan and mix well. Bring to a boil and stir in the rice. Remove from the heat and let stand for 5 to 10 minutes to cool. Press the rice into a round mould. Layer the mangos and avocados over the rice.

For the beef, sprinkle the strip loin on both sides with salt and coat evenly with the crushed peppercorns. Sear on a hot griddle for 1 minute on each side. Cut into thin slices.

To serve, unmould the rice and invert onto a serving platter. Arrange the beef slices in a fan over the top. Drizzle with the dressing and sprinkle with the scallions.

Serves 8   Chef Thong Lee Goh

. The Harbourfront

The Harbourfront is one of Hamilton's most enduring restaurants, offering a classic dinner setting overlooking the harbour. The restaurant also features an award-winning sushi and tempura bar with a popular sushi happy hour. A new grill room was added in 2001, so multiple dining options are available.

The Harbourfront
21 Front Street West
Hamilton
info@harbourfront.bm
441-295-4207

La Coquille
Restaurant & Lounge

Stunning construction and subtle lighting, with a glass verandah overlooking the tranquil waters of the "Foot of the Lane," Hamilton Harbour is home to La Coquille, one of the island's premier restaurants. The menu emphasises southern French cuisine and, under the guidance of its executive chef, has won many awards.

La Coquille

Bermuda Underwater

Exploration Institute

40 Crow Lane East Broadway

Hamilton

info@coquille.bm

441-292-6122

Chilled Tequila Soup
with Strawberries and Green Peppercorns

3 ounces tequila
4 cups fresh strawberries
1 teaspoon green peppercorns
1/2 cup plain yoghurt
2 teaspoons honey
1 cup sweet wine
juice of 1 lime
sliced strawberries

Combine the tequila, 4 cups strawberries, peppercorns, yoghurt, honey, wine and lime juice in a blender. Process until smooth. Chill for 6 hours. Serve in frosted glasses and garnish with additional sliced strawberries.

Serves 6

Truffle and Bean Soup
(Cappuccino Style)

1/2 onion, chopped
1 (16-ounce) can white beans, drained and rinsed
4 cups chicken stock
1 cup heavy cream
salt and pepper to taste
several drops of truffle oil

Sauté the onion in a nonstick saucepan until tender. Add the beans and chicken stock. Bring to a boil and reduce the heat. Simmer for 10 minutes. Process in a blender until smooth. Strain the mixture through muslin into the saucepan and add the cream. Simmer for 5 minutes longer. Season with salt, pepper and truffle oil to taste.

Serves 4

Chef Serge Bottelli

Pollo Cacciatore

(Chicken Hunter Style)

4 pounds chicken breasts or legs
salt and pepper to taste
1/2 cup flour
6 tablespoons olive oil
12 ounces mushrooms
1 green bell pepper, julienned
1 red bell pepper, julienned
1 onion, thinly sliced
2 medium carrots, cut into sticks
4 large garlic cloves, chopped
1/2 cup white wine
1 cup tomato sauce
1 cup chicken broth

Season the chicken with salt and pepper and coat with the flour. Heat the olive oil in a ovenproof saucepan or dish. Add the chicken and sauté until brown on all sides. Remove the chicken to a plate and add the mushrooms, bell peppers, onion, carrots and garlic to the saucepan. Sauté for 6 to 8 minutes or until the vegetables are tender.

Return the chicken to the saucepan and add the wine. Cook until the wine evaporates. Stir in the tomato sauce and chicken broth.

Place in an oven preheated to 350 degrees. Bake for 45 to 60 minutes or until the chicken is tender and cooked through. Serve with boiled or roasted small potatoes and a green vegetable.

Serves 8   *Chef Angelo d'Amato*

Loved by locals and visitors alike, this is the very definition of a festive trattoria. It is conveniently located in central Hamilton, with the Island's only wood-burning pizza oven as a centrepiece, and serves great pizza, pasta, and fun for the whole family.

La Trattoria
Washington Lane
Hamilton
info@trattoria.bm
441-295-1877

Maine Lobster Salad

with Celery, Basil and Lemon Dressing

CELERY, BASIL AND LEMON DRESSING

2 ribs celery, chopped
1 bunch basil leaves
1 bunch spinach leaves
1 tablespoon pine nuts
1/2 cup lemon juice
3 tablespoons olive oil
2 tablespoons raspberry vinegar
1 tablespoon honey
salt and pepper to taste

LOBSTER TEMPURA

1 Maine lobster tail, cut into
  large strips
lemon juice
tempura flour
salt and pepper to taste
oil for deep-frying

LOBSTER SALAD

tail and claw meat of 1 boiled
  Maine lobster
1 mango, julienned
2 tomatoes, peeled, seeded and
  julienned
1 bunch asparagus, boiled and
  julienned
1 rib celery, julienned
1 tablespoon pine nuts
1 teaspoon lemon juice
1 teaspoon lime juice
1 teaspoon truffle oil
1 teaspoon sesame oil
salt and pepper to taste
chopped fresh chives or Italian
  parsley

For the dressing, combine all the ingredients in a blender and process until smooth. Chill until serving time.

For the lobster tempura, combine the lobster with lemon juice in a bowl and toss to coat well. Let stand for 15 minutes; drain. Mix tempura flour with enough ice water to make a smooth batter in a bowl. Season with salt and pepper. Dip the lobster into the batter and deep-fry in 325- to 350-degree oil until golden brown.

For the salad, combine the lobster meat with the mango, tomatoes, asparagus, celery and pine nuts in a bowl. Add the lemon juice, lime juice, truffle oil, sesame oil, salt and pepper and mix gently.

To serve, spoon 2 tablespoons of the dressing onto each serving plate and top with some of the lobster salad. Add 2 strips of the lobster tempura to each plate and top with fresh chives.

Serves 4

Chef Danny Lim

Roasted Duck

(Szechwanese Style)

1 tablespoon hoisin sauce
4 to 6 tablespoons Chinese cooking wine (optional)
2 pieces star anise
1/2 gingerroot, peeled and sliced
1 scallion, chopped
2 tablespoons Chinese five-spice powder
1 teaspoon sugar
1 teaspoon salt
1 (4- to 5-pound) duck
1 cup vinegar
1 cup sugar
1/2 teaspoon red food colouring (optional)

Combine the hoisin sauce, wine, star anise, gingerroot, scallion, five-spice powder, 1 teaspoon sugar, and salt in a bowl and mix well for the marinade. Rub the mixture under the skin and inside the cavity of the duck. Close the cavity with a bamboo skewer or tie the legs with twine.

Bring enough water to cover the duck to a boil in a large saucepan. Add the vinegar, 1 cup sugar and food colouring and stir to dissolve the sugar. Add the duck and boil for 20 seconds. Remove from the liquid and let stand in the refrigerator for 3 to 4 hours or until the skin is dry and firm.

Place in a roasting pan and roast at 450 degrees for 45 minutes. Serve with hoisin sauce or plum sauce and vegetables.

Serves 2 to 4   *Chef Danny Lim*

L'Oriental is Hamilton's premier Asian restaurant, boasting the Island's first Asian fusion cuisine. Whether you dine in the main restaurant under the pagoda, at the teppanyaki table, the sushi bar, or on the outside terrace, this restaurant is a "must."

L'Oriental
32 Bermudiana Road
Hamilton
info@loriental.bm
441-296-4477

The Lobster Pot is known for its fine seafood and warm, friendly service. Guests of the restaurant enjoy its casual atmosphere and engaging hospitality over lunch, dinner, or cocktails. Lobster is prepared to taste at the Lobster Pot.

The Seafood Feast for Two is a hearty medley of lobster, mussels, clams, crab claws, and shrimp simmered in a saffron bouillon.

Island Conch Chowder

3 tablespoons olive oil
1/2 cup chopped onion
1/2 cup chopped celery
1/2 cup chopped bell pepper
1/2 cup chopped carrot
2 tablespoons salt
1 tablespoon white pepper
1 tablespoon chopped garlic
1 1/2 pounds conch meat, minced
1/2 cup white wine
3 tablespoons curry powder
1 tablespoon jerk seasoning
1 teaspoon fresh or dried thyme leaves
2 bay leaves
2 quarts chicken stock
1 cup flour
1/2 cup heavy cream

Heat the olive oil in a sauté pan. Add the onion, celery, bell pepper, carrot, salt and white pepper; sauté lightly. Add the garlic, conch meat and wine and simmer for 5 minutes. Season with the curry powder, jerk seasoning, thyme leaves and bay leaves.

Stir in the chicken stock and bring to a boil. Reduce the heat and simmer for 30 minutes. Blend the flour with enough water to make a smooth mixture the consistency of pancake batter. Add to the chowder and simmer until thickened, stirring constantly. Simmer for 5 minutes longer. Add the cream and adjust the seasonings; discard the bay leaves.

Serves 12

Coconut Shrimp

2 tablespoons soy sauce
1 tablespoon lemon juice
1 teaspoon finely chopped garlic
1/2 teaspoon salt
1/2 teaspoon crushed pepper
1 1/2 pounds tiger shrimp, peeled and deveined
1 cup flour
4 eggs, beaten
16 ounces flaked sweetened coconut
oil for deep-frying

Combine the soy sauce, lemon juice, garlic, salt and pepper in a bowl and mix well. Add the shrimp and toss to coat well. Marinate in the refrigerator for 2 hours. Coat the shrimp with the flour, shaking off any excess. Dip in the beaten egg and roll in the coconut, coating well. Chill in the refrigerator for 1 hour.

Deep-fry in 350-degree oil until golden brown. Remove to a paper towel with a slotted spoon to drain. Serve on a bed of summer greens tossed in a vinaigrette and add a sweet chile dipping sauce.

Serves 6

The hearty appetites of landlubbers appreciate the rack of lamb, grilled chicken, or filet mignon.

The selection of delicious and imaginative salads and sandwiches are favoured lighter fare at the Lobster Pot.

The Lobster Pot
6 Bermudiana Road
Hamilton
lobsterpot@ibl.bm
441-292-6898

Pink Beach

C L U B

TUCKER'S TOWN · BERMUDA

Evening dining at Pink Beach is a delightful experience. Whatever your menu selection, the chef creatively combines the freshest ingredients, resulting in wonderful taste sensations complemented by a colourful and exotic presentation that is pleasing to both the palate and the eye.

The Breakers Ocean Terrace is open for a relaxed lunch or dinner and provides a casual and relaxed bistro atmosphere. There is a wide range of dishes to choose from, with an emphasis on seafood. Poolside buffet barbeques are often held, and a calypso band provides entertainment.

Sashimi Tuna Spring Rolls
with a Fennel and Orange Slaw

FENNEL AND ORANGE SLAW

1 bulb fennel, thinly sliced
sections of 1 orange
1/4 cup sesame oil
2 tablespoons rice vinegar
2 tablespoons black sesame seeds
salt and pepper to taste

SASHIMI TUNA SPRING ROLLS

4 spring roll wrappers or pastry
  sheets
4 ounces spinach leaves, julienned
salt and pepper to taste
1 teaspoon toasted white sesame
  seeds
3 tablespoons sweet soy sauce
4 (1 1/2×4-inch) pieces sashimi tuna
1/4 cup cornstarch
1/4 cup cold water
vegetable oil for deep-frying
orange sections and fresh herbs

For the slaw, combine all the ingredients in a bowl and toss to mix well.

For the spring rolls, arrange the spring roll wrappers on a work surface with 1 point toward you. Spread the spinach on the wrappers, leaving 1/2 inch on all sides. Season with salt and pepper.

Mix the sesame seeds with 1 tablespoon of the sweet soy sauce. Roll the tuna in the seed mixture, coating evenly. Place on the wrappers and brush the edges with a mixture of the cornstarch and water. Roll the wrappers halfway, starting at the nearest point. Fold the sides into the middle and roll to completely enclose the filling; press the edges to seal.

Heat vegetable oil to 350 degrees and add the spring rolls. Deep-fry until the wrappers are golden brown, but the tuna is still rare. Remove from the oil with a slotted spoon and drain on paper towels. Cut into halves on a deep diagonal.

To serve, spoon the slaw onto 4 serving plates. Arrange the spring roll halves on the plates. Sprinkle with additional orange sections and fresh herbs. Drizzle with the remaining sweet soy sauce.

Serves 4   *Executive Chef Joanne Bainbridge*

Pan-Seared Sea Bass

on Creamy Beet Root Risotto

CREAMY BEET ROOT RISOTTO

28 ounces light chicken stock
1 large Bermuda onion, minced
2 garlic cloves, finely chopped
2 sprigs of thyme
2 tablespoons olive oil
11 ounces uncooked arborio rice
2 beet roots, cooked and cut into
   1/4-inch pieces
4 ounces white wine
2 ounces Parmesan cheese, grated
4 tablespoons unsalted butter
salt and pepper to taste
6 ounces heavy cream

PAN-SEARED SEA BASS

2 tablespoons olive oil
4 (6-ounce) skin-on sea bass fillets,
   scored
4 ounces heavy cream
2 ounces unsalted butter, chopped
2 tablespoons lemon juice
4 ounces cooked spinach, heated
edible flowers or herbs

For the risotto, heat the chicken stock in a medium saucepan and keep warm. Sauté the onion, garlic and thyme in the olive oil in a large saucepan until the onion is tender. Add the rice and 1 of the beet roots. Add the wine and 1/3 of the heated stock, stirring to deglaze the saucepan. Cook until reduced by 1/3. Add half the remaining stock and simmer until the liquid has been absorbed. Add the remaining stock, Parmesan cheese, butter, salt and pepper. Simmer until the rice is cooked al dente. Keep warm. Stir in the cream and the remaining beet root just before serving; adjust the seasonings.

For the sea bass, heat the olive oil in an ovenproof sauté pan. Add the sea bass skin side down and pan-fry until light brown. Place in an oven preheated to 350 degrees and bake for 6 to 8 minutes or until the fish flakes easily. Heat a saucepan over high heat. Add the cream and bring just to a simmer. Whisk in the butter gradually. Whisk in the lemon juice.

To serve, spoon the risotto onto 4 serving plates. Place the sea bass fillets on the rice and top with the spinach. Drizzle the butter sauce around the fish. Garnish with edible flowers or herbs.

Serves 4

Executive Chef Joanne Bainbridge

The Bermudiana Dining Room at the Pink Beach Club presents the perfect setting to enjoy a gastronomic five-course dinner with a menu that changes daily. There are more than 200 wines on the extensive wine list. The meal is complemented by an exquisite selection of desserts and cheeses. Enjoy a specialty coffee or adjourn to the terrace to enjoy cigars and liqueurs, followed by dancing until 11:30. It also includes nightly entertainment in the dining room and the terrace from April to October.

Pink Beach Club
South Road
Smith Parish
Tucker's Town
www.pinkbeachclub.com
441-293-1666

This intimate restaurant is one of Bermuda's most popular spots for lunch five days a week or for dinner nightly. Set amid the hustle and bustle of Front Street, it is an oasis of fine cuisine for dining inside or on the al fresco harbour-view terrace. Award-winning signature dishes feature contemporary styles with an emphasis on fresh Bermuda seafood. Enjoy the comfortable, casual atmosphere and professional service with a selection from the "Wine Spectator" award-winning wine list that showcases more than 50 wines by the glass.

Port O' Call

87 Front Street

Hamilton

www.portocall.bm

441-295-5373

Yellowfin Tuna
with Sake-Braised Shiitakes

caps of 1 pound shiitake mushrooms
1 teaspoon sesame oil
1 cup sake
1 cup rice wine vinegar
4 cups chicken stock
2/3 pound new potatoes
1 cup (4 ounces) crumbled goat
    cheese
4 ounces (1 stick) butter

1 cup milk, heated
sea salt and freshly ground pepper
    to taste
24 asparagus spears
olive oil
6 (6- to 8-ounce) tuna steaks
2 cups sesame seeds
chili powder or dried chile flakes
    to taste

Toss the mushroom caps with the sesame oil in a bowl. Let stand for 3 minutes. Heat a heavy sauté pan over medium heat. Add the mushrooms and sauté until seared. Stir in the sake and rice wine vinegar and increase the heat to high. Cook until reduced by 1/4. Add the chicken stock and reduce the heat to low. Simmer for 15 to 25 minutes or until the mushrooms are tender.

Scrub the potatoes and cook in their skins in enough water to cover in a saucepan for 15 to 20 minutes or until tender; drain. Add the goat cheese, butter and hot milk to the saucepan and mash, leaving enough lumps to give texture; season with sea salt and pepper.

Brush the asparagus with olive oil and season with sea salt and pepper. Grill for 3 to 4 minutes or until tender.

Brush both sides of the tuna steaks with olive oil and season with sea salt and pepper. Press the sesame seeds and chili powder over both sides. Sear in a heavy preheated skillet for 1 minute on each side.

Mound the mashed potatoes onto 6 serving plates. Slice the tuna steaks into halves diagonally and place on the potatoes. Add the asparagus and spoon the mushrooms with their cooking juices around the edges of the plates.

Serves 6

Vanilla Panna Cotta

with Blackberry Compote

VANILLA PANNA COTTA

1 tablespoon unflavoured gelatin
3 tablespoons water
4 cups heavy cream
2/3 cup sugar
1 vanilla bean, split lengthwise

BLACKBERRY COMPOTE

1 tablespoon unsalted butter
2 cups blackberries
1/3 cup sugar
cassis to taste
1/2 teaspoon ginger
1/2 teaspoon cinnamon

For the panna cotta, soften the gelatin in the water in a small bowl for 1 minute; do not stir. Combine the cream, sugar and vanilla bean in a medium saucepan and bring to a simmer over medium heat, stirring to dissolve the sugar.

Remove from the heat and add the gelatin mixture, stirring to dissolve the gelatin completely. Return to the heat if the gelatin does not dissolve completely within 3 minutes and warm gently, stirring constantly until the gelatin dissolves. Remove the vanilla bean and pour into 6 to 8 ramekins or dessert cups. Chill, uncovered, for 2 hours.

For the compote, melt the butter in a large sauté pan over high heat and cook until bubbly. Add the blackberries and sauté for 2 minutes. Stir in the sugar and liqueur and cook for 2 minutes or until the sugar dissolves, stirring constantly. Remove from the heat and allow flames to die down if the liqueur should ignite.

Add the ginger and cinnamon and mix well. Cook for 2 to 3 minutes longer. Remove from the heat and cool for 5 minutes.

To serve, dip the bottoms of the ramekins into hot water for 10 seconds and invert the panna cotta onto dessert plates. Spoon the compote around the panna cotta. You may also serve the panna cotta in the ramekins if preferred.

Serves 6 to 8

Tucked away in one of Hamilton's most enchanting and historical alleys, Bistro J offers a unique, wholesome, and imaginative menu that changes every day. Served in a lively bistro setting, the daily specials include fresh local seafood, the finest European and American meats, homemade pastas, and award-winning desserts. The wine list is extensive and features wines by the glass or bottle. Open for lunch five days a week and dinner nightly, this culinary jewel is a must for those wishing to enjoy modestly priced dining in a vibrant atmosphere.

Bistro J
Chancery Lane
Hamilton
www.bistroj.bm
441-296-8546

THE TASTES OF

COCKTAILS & CANAPÉS

BREAKFAST & BRUNCH

SOUPS & SALADS

ENTRÉES

ON THE SIDE

DESSERTS

Bermuda

Cocktails & Canapés

Bermuda Rum Swizzle

96 ounces (12 cups) pineapple juice
10 ounces (1¼ cups) orange juice
juice of 4 lemons
juice of 4 limes
40 ounces (5 cups) Barbados rum
40 ounces (5 cups) Goslings Black Seal rum or
   other dark rum

6 ounces (¾ cup) brandy
8 drops of Angostura bitters
Bermuda Falernum or simple sugar syrup to taste
46 ounces (5¾ cups) water
½ cup sugar
nutmeg to taste

Combine the pineapple juice and orange juice in a large container and add the lemon juice and lime juice. Stir in most of the rums and brandy, reserving a small amount of each to adjust the taste. Add the bitters, Falernum, water and sugar and stir to dissolve the sugar completely. Adjust the flavour with the rums, brandy, Falernum and sugar.

Pour back into the empty rum bottles or other sealable containers and seal. Chill until serving time. Serve over ice and garnish with a sprinkle of nutmeg if desired.

Serves 36

Dawn Dunstan

Champagne Punch with a Punch

6 ounces (3/4 cup) frozen grapefruit concentrate, thawed
12 ounces (1 1/2 cups) frozen orange juice concentrate, thawed
26 ounces (3 1/4 cups) club soda
2 bottles of Champagne
26 ounces (3 1/4 cups) apricot brandy, or to taste

Combine the grapefruit juice concentrate, orange juice concentrate and club soda in a large punch bowl and mix well. Add the Champagne and brandy to taste and mix gently. Add enough ice to chill.

Serves 20 to 30

Kim Paterson

Chilled Irish Cream

4 eggs
1 (14-ounce) can sweetened condensed milk
12 ounces (1 1/2 cups) blended whisky
1 tablespoon chocolate syrup
1/2 teaspoon instant coffee granules
1 teaspoon vanilla extract
1/2 teaspoon coconut extract
1/8 teaspoon almond extract

Combine the eggs, sweetened condensed milk and whisky in a blender. Add the chocolate syrup, coffee granules, vanilla extract, coconut extract and almond extract; process for 2 minutes. Pour into a bottle and store in the refrigerator. Shake gently before serving.

To avoid raw eggs that may carry salmonella, use an equivalent amount of pasteurized egg substitute.

Makes almost 1 quart

Erin Anderson

Island Cocktails

Banana Daiquiri: Combine ⅓ ripe banana, 1 teaspoon sugar, 1 tablespoon lime or lemon juice, 3 tablespoons Bacardi® light rum and ½ cup ice in a blender. Process for 10 to 20 seconds or until smooth. Pour into a chilled cocktail glass to serve.

Limón Cosmo: Combine ¼ cup Bacardi Limón®, 2 tablespoons Triple Sec, 1 tablespoon lime juice, ¼ cup cranberry juice and a handful of ice in a cocktail shaker. Shake well and pour into a salt-rimmed margarita glass to serve.

Mojito: Combine 12 mint leaves in a Collins glass and crush well. Add 2 dashes of bitters and and the juice of ½ lime. Add 2 teaspoons simple syrup or add 4 teaspoons sugar. Fill nearly to the top of the glass with ice and add 3 tablespoons Bacardi® light rum. Top off with club soda and mix well. Garnish with additional sprigs of mint or a slice of lime.

Whisky Sour: Combine 3 tablespoons Dewar's White Label® and 3 tablespoons whisky sour mix in a highball glass and mix well. Add ice and mix to chill.

Loquat Liqueur

¹/₃ gallon ripe loquats
¹/₃ gallon super-fine castor sugar
¹/₃ gallon pure ethyl alcohol

Cut the tops and bottoms from the loquats; do not remove the seeds. Place in a 1-gallon jar with a tight-fitting lid, filling ¹/₃ full. Add the sugar, filling ²/₃ full. Add the alcohol, filling to within 1 inch of the top. Seal the jar and invert to shake gently until the sugar dissolves. Let stand for 6 months, shaking the jar once each week. Remove the fruit, allow the liqueur to settle and strain to serve.

Makes ¹/₂ gallon   Deborah Titterton Narraway

Holiday Eggnog

2 quarts vanilla ice cream, softened
1 quart hot strong coffee
1 quart cream or milk
12 eggs
rum to taste
grated nutmeg

Combine the ice cream, coffee and cream in small batches in a blender, adding 2 to 3 eggs to each batch and processing each batch until smooth. Combine the mixtures in a large punch bowl. Add rum to taste. Garnish the servings with grated nutmeg.

To avoid raw eggs that may carry salmonella, use an equivalent amount of pasteurized egg substitute.

Makes 3 to 4 quarts   Cornelia Kempe

SIMPLE SUGAR SYRUP

Combine 1 cup sugar, 1 cup water and ¹/₈ teaspoon cream of tartar in a saucepan. Bring to a simmer, stirring until the sugar dissolves and brushing down the side of the saucepan with a pastry brush to remove any sugar crystals. Simmer for 5 minutes longer and remove from the heat to cool completely. Store, covered, in the refrigerator for up to 3 months. Use for cocktails or other recipes.

Party Crostini

8 ounces cream cheese, softened
1 cup (4 ounces) crumbled feta cheese
1/2 cup milk
1 baguette French bread

1 (7-ounce) jar oil-pack sun-dried tomatoes
1 small Bermuda onion, chopped
1/4 cup capers
3 tablespoons minced garlic

Combine the cream cheese, feta cheese and milk in a bowl and mix until smooth. Chill in the refrigerator.

Cut the French bread into 1/4-inch slices. Remove half the sun-dried tomatoes from the jar to a bowl, reserving the remaining sun-dried tomatoes for another use. Brush both sides of the bread slices lightly with the oil remaining in the jar and arrange the slices on a baking sheet. Bake at 400 degrees for 4 minutes on each side.

Add the onion, capers and garlic to the sun-dried tomatoes in the bowl. Spoon the cheese mixture onto the crostini and drizzle with the sun-dried tomato mixture. Serve warm.

Makes 2 to 3 dozen

wendi Ryland

Chicken Satay
with Peanut Dipping Sauce

CHICKEN

2 garlic cloves, crushed
1 (1-inch) piece gingerroot, peeled and grated
2 tablespoons sherry
2 tablespoons light soy sauce
1 tablespoon white wine vinegar
1 tablespoon sesame oil
1 pound boneless skinless chicken breasts

PEANUT DIPPING SAUCE

2 tablespoons smooth peanut butter
2 tablespoons chopped unsalted peanuts
1 tablespoon light soy sauce
1 tablespoon lime juice or lemon juice
2 teaspoons honey
2 tablespoons coconut milk

For the chicken, combine the garlic, gingerroot, sherry, soy sauce, vinegar and sesame oil in a shallow dish and mix well to form a marinade. Cut the chicken across the grain into thin strips. Add to the marinade and mix to coat well. Marinate in the refrigerator for 8 hours or longer. Soak bamboo skewers in water for 30 minutes or longer. Drain the chicken and bamboo skewers. Thread the chicken onto the skewers.

For the dipping sauce, combine the peanut butter, peanuts, soy sauce, lime juice, honey and coconut milk in a food processor and process until smooth. Spoon into a saucepan and cook over low heat just until heated through. Adjust the amounts of coconut milk or peanut butter if necessary for the desired consistency.

Grill the chicken over hot coals for 4 minutes. Turn and grill for 4 minutes longer or until cooked through. Serve with the warm peanut sauce for dipping.

Serves 4 to 6

Louise Gibbons

SECURITY ADVICE FOR WOMEN *The BJSL sponsored a pamphlet, produced by the Bermuda Police Service, on women's security.*

Cheese Cookies

2 cups (8 ounces) shredded sharp Cheddar cheese
1 cup (2 sticks) margarine or butter, softened
2 cups flour
2 cups crisp rice cereal, finely crushed
6 to 10 drops of hot pepper sauce
$1/2$ teaspoon paprika
$3/4$ teaspoon salt
$1/2$ teaspoon cayenne pepper

Combine the cheese and margarine in a blender, food processor or large bowl. Add the flour, cereal, pepper sauce, paprika, salt and cayenne pepper and process or mix until well combined. Shape into 1-inch balls and place on an ungreased baking sheet. Press each with the thumb to flatten slightly. Bake at 350 degrees for 4 to 5 minutes or until golden brown.

Makes about 3 dozen   *Barbara Cooper*

Gougère

6 tablespoons ($3/4$ stick) butter
1 cup water
1 teaspoon salt
pepper to taste
1 cup flour
4 eggs
1 cup (4 ounces) shredded Gruyère or Swiss cheese

Melt the butter in a saucepan. Add the water, salt and pepper and bring to a boil. Add the flour all at once and cook until the mixture forms a ball, stirring constantly. Place in a food processor and add the eggs 1 at a time, mixing well after each addition. Add the cheese and process until smooth.

Spoon the mixture onto baking sheets by rounded teaspoonfuls. Freeze for several hours. Remove to plastic bags and store in the freezer. Place while still frozen on a baking sheet and bake at 400 degrees for 15 minutes or until golden brown.

Makes 6 dozen   *Sally Gibbons*

Crab and Cream Cheese Tarts

1 sheet frozen pastry, thawed
1 (6-ounce) can crab meat, drained
2 tablespoons thinly sliced scallions
2 tablespoons mayonnaise
8 ounces cream cheese, softened

1/2 cup (2 ounces) shredded Cheddar cheese
2 tablespoons grated Parmesan cheese
1 teaspoon Worcestershire sauce
paprika to taste

Cut the pastry into circles and press into greased miniature tart or tartlet cups. Combine the crab meat, scallions, mayonnaise, cream cheese, Cheddar cheese, Parmesan cheese and Worcestershire sauce in a large bowl and mix well. Spoon into the prepared tart cups and spread evenly. Sprinkle with paprika.

Bake at 375 degrees on the center oven rack for 15 to 20 minutes or until light brown; turn the muffin pans frequently to prevent overbrowning. Serve warm or at room temperature.

You may also use unbaked phyllo cups or one 16-ounce can of refrigerator crescent roll dough or biscuit dough for the tart shells. Divide the dough for each crescent roll or biscuit into halves and press into the tart pans. You may also freeze the tarts.

Makes 2 dozen

Paula Dilney-Friend

ISLAND CONCH

Found in southern waters, conch is known for its beautiful and brightly coloured spiral shell. The foot-shaped muscle is delicious fresh but is also available canned or frozen. Conch can be eaten uncooked in salads or used in chowder and pies.

The peak season for conch is summer, although it is highly protected in Bermuda's waters. Under the Fisheries (Protected Species) Order 1978, the Queen Conch (Strombus Gigas) and the Harbour Conch (Strombus Costatus) are illegal to import and an offence to purchase, possess, or take from Bermuda waters.

Conch Fritters

ISLAND TARTAR SAUCE

1/4 cup mayonnaise
1 tablespoon pickled jalapeño slices, drained and chopped
1 tablespoon minced red onion
1 tablespoon chopped fresh cilantro
1 tablespoon fresh lime juice

FRITTERS

1 1/2 cups flour
2 teaspoons baking powder
1/2 teaspoon ginger
pinch of nutmeg
1/2 teaspoon salt
1/2 teaspoon freshly ground pepper
1 egg, lightly beaten
2/3 cup milk
1 Bermuda onion, chopped
1 small garlic clove, minced
1 tomato, peeled and chopped
1 green bell pepper, or 1 or 2 jalapeño chiles, seeded and chopped
1 pound uncooked conch meat, cut into chunks
salt and pepper to taste
oil for deep-frying
lime wedges

For the tartar sauce, combine the mayonnaise, jalapeño slices, onion, cilantro and lime juice in a bowl and mix well. Chill, covered, until serving time.

For the fritters, sift the flour, baking powder, ginger, nutmeg, 1/2 teaspoon salt and 1/2 teaspoon pepper into a large mixing bowl. Make a well in the center and add the egg and half the milk; mix well. Add the rest of the milk, onion, garlic, tomato and green pepper gradually, beating just until mixed; do not overbeat.

Pat the conch dry and season with salt and pepper to taste. Dip into the batter, coating well. Deep-fry in heated oil for 2 to 3 minutes or until golden brown; drain on paper towels. Serve with the tartar sauce and lime wedges.

Serves 4 to 6   *Deborah Titterton Narraway*

Smoked Salmon Tortilla Rolls

2 ounces cream cheese, softened
1/2 red onion, finely chopped
2 tablespoons capers

2 teaspoons caper juice
3 flour tortillas
4 ounces smoked salmon, sliced

Combine the cream cheese, onion, capers and caper juice in a bowl and mix well. Let stand at room temperature until easily spread. Spread evenly on the tortillas, leaving the edges bare. Arrange the salmon over the cream cheese mixture. Roll the tortillas tightly to enclose the filling.

Wrap the rolls individually in plastic wrap, twisting the ends to seal. Chill for 3 hours or longer. Cut diagonally into pieces to serve.

Serves 6

Jacqui Horsfield

Cocktail Fish Cakes with Banana

1¹/2 pounds boneless salted codfish
5 pounds potatoes, peeled
¹/2 cup chopped parsley
1 small onion, chopped
2 tablespoons thyme
salt and pepper to taste
1 or 2 eggs (optional)
8 large bananas
vegetable oil for frying

Soak the codfish in enough water to cover in a bowl for 8 hours or longer. Drain and cover with enough fresh water to cover in a saucepan. Bring to a boil and boil for several minutes; drain. Cool the fish and flake into a bowl.

Combine the potatoes with enough water to cover in a saucepan. Cook until tender; drain. Remove the potatoes to a bowl and mash until smooth. Add the flaked fish, parsley, onion, thyme, salt and pepper and mix well. Add 1 or 2 eggs if necessary for the desired consistency.

Shape the mixture into balls with a 1-ounce ice cream scoop and flatten lightly. Fry in heated oil in a skillet until golden brown. Drain on paper towels. Cut the bananas into ¹/4-inch slices and secure 1 to each codfish cake with wooden picks.

Makes 60 to 70

Franz Wolmuth,
Executive Chef, Bank of Bermuda

Stuffed Mushroom Caps

2 tablespoons chopped Bermuda onion
1/2 cup (2 ounces) crumbled blue cheese
8 ounces cream cheese, softened
24 small mushrooms

Combine the onion, blue cheese and cream cheese in a bowl and mix well. Spoon the mixture into the mushroom caps. Arrange on a baking sheet. Broil for 1 to 2 minutes or until the cheese melts and the tops are brown.

Serves 12   *Kim Paterson*

CLEANING MUSHROOMS

Mushrooms soak up water like a sponge, then release it later in the cooking process. This can change the consistency of the recipe, so try "dry cleaning" your favourite fungi. You can find a mushroom brush with soft bristles at most kitchen stores. Moisten the brush or a cloth lightly with water and gently wipe the mushrooms clean.

ISLAND COCKTAILS

Coral Cocktail:
combine 3 tablespoons
light rum, 1 tablespoon
lemon or lime juice,
1 tablespoon grapefruit
juice and 1 tablespoon
apricot brandy with ice
in a cocktail shaker or
blender. Shake or process
until well mixed and
chilled. Strain into a
cocktail glass to serve.

Bermudian Shandy:
combine 1 bottle of lager
beer with a can of ginger
beer or lemon–lime soda
over ice in a glass and
mix well.

Bermuda Rose:
Pour 1/4 cup gin,
2 tablespoons apricot
brandy, 2 tablespoons
grenadine and
2 tablespoons lemon
juice over ice in a
glass and mix well.

Melon and Mozzarella
with Prosciutto

1 ripe cantaloupe
8 to 10 water-pack small fresh mozzarella balls, drained
20 to 24 slices paper-thin prosciutto, cut into 1×3-inch strips
lemon juice or lime juice
freshly ground pepper

Cut the cantaloupe into halves and discard the seeds. Scoop the cantaloupe into balls with a melon baller. Chill the melon balls and mozzarella balls in the refrigerator until serving time.

Wrap the mozzarella and melon with strips of prosciutto and secure with wooden picks. Sprinkle with lemon juice and pepper. Arrange on a serving platter and serve immediately.

You may also use the larger mozzarella balls and cut them into 1/2×2-inch sticks.

Makes 30   *Mollie Meyer*

Paw Paw Fritters

1 cup self-rising flour
1/2 cup milk
1 egg, beaten
1 1/2 tablespoons sugar
1 cup chopped peeled paw paw
oil for deep-frying

Combine the flour, milk, egg and sugar in a medium bowl and mix well. Add the paw paw and mix gently by hand; do not overmix. Drop the mixture by teaspoonful in hot oil and deep-fry for 1 to 2 minutes on each side or until golden brown. Drain on paper towels. Serve hot as an appetiser or as a side dish.

Select a paw paw that is slightly underripe with greenish-yellow or greenish-orange skin for the best results. You may also prepare the fritters by spooning the batter onto a griddle and cooking as you would pancakes.

Makes 8   *Deborah Titterton Narraway*

DARK 'N' STORMY

To enjoy one of Bermuda's most popular cocktails, pour 3 tablespoons Goslings Black Seal® rum into a glass filled with ice. Top with Barritts Ginger Beer® to taste and garnish with a lemon slice. Increase the amounts to make a pitcher to share with friends.

Devilled Eggs

12 eggs
salt to taste
5 tablespoons mayonnaise
2 tablespoons mustard

1 tablespoon chopped parsley
pepper to taste
paprika

Cook the eggs in salted boiling water in a saucepan. Drain and remove to a bowl of ice to cool. Peel the eggs and cut into halves lengthwise; remove the yolks to a bowl, reserving the whites. Add the mayonnaise, mustard and parsley to the yolks and mash until smooth. Season with salt and pepper to taste. Spoon or pipe the mixture into the egg whites. Arrange on a serving plate and cover well. Chill for 1 hour or longer before serving. Sprinkle with paprika to serve.

Cooking the eggs in the salted boiling water and cooling in the bowl of ice makes them easy to peel.

Makes 2 dozen

Deborah Titterton Narraway

Fresh Guacamole

2 Bermuda avocados
2 ripe medium tomatoes, finely chopped
1 small Bermuda onion, grated
2 scallions, finely chopped
1 garlic clove, minced
2 tablespoons chopped green chile or jalapeño chile
2 to 4 teaspoons fresh lime juice
1 teaspoon olive oil
1/2 teaspoon chili powder or ground cayenne pepper
1 teaspoon salt
1 teaspoon pepper

Mash the avocados in a medium bowl. Add the tomato, onion, scallions, garlic, chile, lime juice and olive oil and mix well. Season with the chili powder, salt and pepper, adjusting the amounts to taste. Spoon into a serving bowl and serve with tortilla chips.

Serves 8 to 10   *Elizabeth Zalinger*

Chile Chicken Dip

8 ounces light cream cheese
1/3 cup low-fat milk
1 cup shredded cooked chicken
1 (4-ounce) can chopped green chiles, drained
1 teaspoon chili powder
1/2 teaspoon salt

Place the cream cheese in a microwave-safe bowl. Microwave on Medium just until softened. Add the milk and mix until smooth. Stir in the chicken, green chiles, chili powder and salt. Microwave on Medium for 2 minutes, stirring occasionally. Microwave for 30 seconds longer or until heated through. Serve warm with tortilla chips.

Serves 8 to 10   *Diane Steiger*

BERMUDA AVOCADO

The type of avocado cultivated in Bermuda is green with a smooth skin and grows twice as large as other avocados. A traditional Bermudian breakfast of codfish and potatoes would not be complete without a complement of sliced fresh avocado; it is also often served in salsas and salads to accompany fresh local fish.

Hot Artichoke and Spinach Dip

1 (16-ounce) can artichokes hearts
2 (10-ounce) packages frozen chopped spinach, thawed
1 cup sour cream
1 cup mayonnaise
1 cup (4 ounces) grated Parmesan cheese
1 envelope vegetable soup mix
garlic salt to taste

Drain and finely chop the artichoke hearts. Press the spinach to remove the excess liquid. Layer the artichokes and half the spinach in a baking dish. Combine the sour cream, mayonnaise, half the Parmesan cheese and vegetable soup mix in a bowl and mix well. Spread over the spinach. Top with the remaining spinach and sprinkle with the remaining Parmesan cheese and garlic salt.

Bake at 350 degrees for 20 to 25 minutes. Stir and serve with water crackers or tortilla chips.

Serves 8

Wendi Ryland

Clam Dip

8 ounces cream cheese, softened
2 tablespoons mayonnaise
1 (6 1/2-ounce) can minced clams, drained
2 to 3 tablespoons finely chopped Bermuda onion
2 or 3 garlic cloves, minced

Combine the cream cheese and mayonnaise in a bowl and mix until smooth. Add the clams, onion and garlic and mix well. Chill for several hours before serving.

Serves 6

Amy Stone

Hot Mushroom Dip

1/2 cup olive oil
1 pound mushrooms, sliced
1 tablespoon flour
1 envelope onion soup mix
1 cup light sour cream
1 cup (4 ounces) shredded cheese
paprika to taste

Heat the olive oil in a heavy ovenproof saucepan with a lid. Add the mushrooms and cook, covered, until tender but not brown, stirring occasionally. Stir in the flour and cook for 2 minutes. Add the onion soup mix and sour cream; mix well. Cook until thickened, stirring constantly. Top with the cheese and sprinkle with paprika.

Bake at 350 degrees for 20 to 30 minutes or until bubbly. Serve with crackers, pita rounds or French bread.

Use the regular size soup mix rather than the cup of soup size for this recipe.

Serves 8   *Jane Spurling*

Antipasto

1 (15-ounce) bottle of chili sauce
1 (15-ounce) bottle of ketchup
juice of 2 lemons
4 to 5 tablespoons horseradish, drained
2 tablespoons Worcestershire sauce
several drops of Tabasco sauce

1 cup finely chopped gherkins
1 small bottle of cocktail onions, drained
1 (10-ounce) can button mushrooms, chopped
1 cup olive-stuffed pimentos, chopped
3 (3-ounce) cans tuna, drained

Combine the chili sauce, ketchup, lemon juice, horseradish, Worcestershire sauce and Tabasco sauce in a bowl and mix well. Add the gherkins, cocktail onions, mushrooms, pimentos and tuna and mix gently. Store in the refrigerator for up to 1 month. Serve cold with crackers or bagel thins.

Serves 24

Ginnie Cooper-Stewart

76

Festive Taramasalata

8 ounces cream cheese, softened
2 scallions, chopped
fresh chives, chopped, to taste
2 tablespoons freshly squeezed lemon juice
1/4 cup (or more) cream
1 small package (or more) smoked salmon, chopped
2 tablespoons red salmon roe

Combine the cream cheese, scallions, chives and lemon juice in a bowl and mix until smooth. Add enough cream to make the desired consistency. Fold in the smoked salmon and roe very gently. Spoon into a serving bowl and serve with crackers.

You may also spoon small amounts onto toasted baguette slices and top with additional roe and chopped chives.

Serves 12

Sue Hendrick

East Indian Cheese Spread

1/4 cup chopped walnuts
1/2 cup chopped golden raisins
1 cup (4 ounces) shredded Cheddar cheese
8 ounces cream cheese, softened
1/4 cup white wine
1/4 teaspoon curry powder
chopped parsley

Mix the walnuts, raisins and Cheddar cheese in a bowl. Combine the cream cheese, wine and curry powder in a bowl and beat until smooth. Add the walnut mixture and mix well. Line a bowl with waxed paper or plastic wrap and press the mixture into the bowl. Chill for 1 hour or longer. Invert the bowl onto a serving plate and remove the waxed paper. Sprinkle with parsley and serve with crackers.

Serves 20

Carolyn Toogood

Bermuda Beauty:
Combine 3 tablespoons
gin, 2 tablespoons apricot
brandy, 1½ teaspoons
grenadine, 1 teaspoon Triple
Sec, juice of ½ orange, juice
of ½ lemon and 1 teaspoon
icing sugar with several
ice cubes in a cocktail
shaker. Shake well and
strain into a glass filled
halfway with ice.

Bermuda Breeze:
Combine 2 tablespoons
dark rum, 1 tablespoon
coconut rum, 1 tablespoon
banana liqueur,
1 tablespoon apricot
liqueur, 1½ teaspoons
grenadine, 1½ teaspoons
Bermuda honey,
1 tablespoon lemon juice,
2 tablespoons orange juice,
2 tablespoons pineapple
juice and 3 or 4 ice cubes
in a blender. Process until
smooth. Pour over ice in
a tall glass and garnish
with an orange slice and
maraschino cherry.

Baked Brie

1/3 cup chopped cranberries
1/3 cup chopped walnuts
3/4 cup strawberry jam or raspberry jam
3½ ounces goat cheese, softened
1 large wedge of Brie cheese, about 1/4 of a large wheel of cheese
1 sheet frozen puff pastry, thawed
1 egg
milk

Combine the cranberries, walnuts and jam in a bowl and mix well. Spread the goat cheese over the Brie; spread the cranberry mixture over the goat cheese.

Place the sheet of puff pastry on a work surface and place the Brie on the pastry. Blend the egg with a small amount of milk in a cup. Brush over the edges of the pastry and fold the pastry to enclose the cheese. Brush the entire pastry package with the egg mixture. Place on a baking sheet and bake at 425 degrees for 20 minutes.

Serves 8 to 10   *Dawn Dunstan*

Cheddar Cheese Spread

1 onion, chopped
1 tablespoon butter
1 cup mayonnaise
1 cup (4 ounces) shredded sharp Cheddar cheese

Sauté the onion in the butter in a saucepan until translucent. Stir in the mayonnaise and Cheddar cheese. Spoon into a small baking dish and bake at 350 degrees for 20 to 30 minutes or until golden brown. Serve warm with crackers.

Serves 12   *Penny Terceira*

Chutney Cheese Ball

16 ounces cream cheese, softened
1/2 cup chopped scallions
1/2 cup coarsely chopped dry-roasted peanuts
1/2 cup flaked coconut
1 (8-ounce) jar chutney

Combine the cream cheese, scallions and peanuts in a bowl and mix well. Shape into a ball. Pat the coconut over the ball and place on a serving plate. Spoon the chutney over the top and serve with crackers.

Serves 8 to 12   *Wendi Ryland*

Pesto and Sun-Dried Tomato Torta

8 ounces cream cheese, softened
1/2 cup (1 stick) butter, softened
1/2 small onion, chopped

1/2 cup pesto
1/2 cup chopped sun-dried tomatoes
1/2 cup pine nuts, toasted

Combine the cream cheese and butter in a food processor or mixing bowl and process or beat until smooth. Stir in the onion.

Line a 2-cup bowl with plastic wrap and spread 1/3 of the cream cheese mixture in the bottom of the bowl. Layer half the pesto, then half the sun-dried tomatoes over the cream cheese mixture, taking care to spread to the edge. Repeat the layers and top with the remaining cream cheese mixture.

Chill, covered, for 2 to 12 hours. Unmold onto a serving plate and remove the plastic wrap. Press the pine nuts over the surface in a decorative pattern. Serve with crackers or sliced baguette. You may garnish the torta with fresh basil leaves or parsley sprigs if desired.

To easily chop the sun-dried tomatoes or other sticky ingredients, use a pair of kitchen shears sprayed with nonstick cooking spray.

Serves 8

Ardleigh Young

Seafood Spread

8 ounces low-fat cream cheese, softened
1/3 cup skim milk
1 cup ketchup
2 tablespoons horseradish
dash of lemon juice
dash of Worcestershire sauce
1 (4-ounce) can shrimp, drained and chopped
1 (4-ounce) can crab meat, flaked
garlic powder, grated Parmesan cheese and chopped parsley to taste

Blend the cream cheese and skim milk in a bowl. Spread evenly on a serving dish. Cover with plastic wrap and refrigerate for 8 hours.

Mix the ketchup, horseradish, lemon juice and Worcestershire sauce in a bowl until smooth. Spread over the cream cheese mixture. Layer the shrimp and crab meat over the top and sprinkle with garlic powder, Parmesan cheese and parsley. Serve with crackers.

Serves 12

Melanie Holmes

BERMUDIAN COOKERY *In 1974, the BJSL's first cookbook was published. To date, this book has sold more than 250,000 copies.*

A common ingredient in many French dishes, shallots look like a miniature version of their relative, the onion. They have a much milder flavour, however. Shallots keep beautifully in a cool, dark place, such as the refrigerator. When a recipe calls for a small amount of onion, shallots are a convenient substitute. Roasting shallots in the oven produces tender caramelised nuggets with a delicious mild flavour.

Salmon Mousse

1 envelope unflavored gelatin
1/2 cup water
1 envelope chicken bouillon
1 (7-ounce) can red salmon, drained
4 shallots
1/2 cup mayonnaise
2 teaspoons lemon juice
1/2 teaspoon salt
1/4 teaspoon pepper
1/2 cup cream

Sprinkle the gelatin over the water in a saucepan and let stand until softened. Bring to a boil, stirring to dissolve the gelatin completely. Combine with the chicken bouillon in a blender and process for 1 minute to dissolve the gelatin completely. Add the salmon, shallots, mayonnaise, lemon juice, salt and pepper and process for 1 minute. Add the cream and process for 30 seconds longer.

Spoon into a mold or serving dish. Chill until firm. Unmold onto a serving plate and serve with crackers, bread or chopped vegetables.

Serves 8 to 10   *Elizabeth Zalinger*

Shark Hash

1 medium shark with a light cream-coloured liver
1 small hot red chile, chopped (optional)
chopped fresh parsley to taste
chopped fresh thyme to taste

Worcestershire sauce to taste
ground black pepper to taste
mayonnaise

Remove the liver from the shark and reserve. Remove and discard the head and tail. Cut the remaining shark into pieces. Combine with enough water to cover and cook, covered, until the fish flakes easily; drain and cool. Remove and discard the skin, bones and cartilage. Press the fish to remove any moisture and shred. Place the shredded shark meat in a large saucepan. Cook over low heat for several hours until very dry, stirring occasionally.

Cut the reserved liver into pieces. Cook, covered, over low heat in a saucepan until the oil is released. Pour into a strainer over a bowl and allow the oil to drain; reserve the oil and discard the liver. This is best done in a well-ventilated room because of the odors released.

Add ²/₃ cup of the reserved shark oil to the shark. Add the red chile, parsley, thyme, Worcestershire sauce and pepper in a bowl and mix well. Cook until the meat has a fine crumbly consistency. Combine the shark with enough mayonnaise to make the desired consistency in a bowl and mix well. Spoon into a serving bowl and serve with toast points or crackers and hot sauce. Omit the mayonnaise to serve as a side dish.

Makes 4 to 6 cups

Cornelia Kempe

Breakfast & Brunch

Bermuda Codfish Breakfast

1 pound salted codfish
1¹/₂ pounds potatoes, peeled and cut into
  2-inch pieces
1 pound onions, sliced into rings
4 bananas, sliced into halves lengthwise

sliced avocado
cherry tomatoes
salt and pepper to taste
Tomato Sauce (page 87)
Egg Sauce (page 87)

Rinse the codfish several times in fresh water. Combine with enough water to cover in a bowl. Soak for 8 hours or longer. Drain and cover with fresh water in a saucepan. Bring to a boil and reduce the heat. Simmer for 30 minutes; drain.

Combine the potatoes and onions with enough water to cover in a saucepan. Bring to a boil and reduce the heat. Simmer for 10 minutes or until the potatoes are tender; drain.

Arrange the codfish, potatoes, onions, bananas, avocado and cherry tomatoes on a serving plate. Season the potatoes with salt and pepper; garnish with parsley. Serve with Tomato Sauce or Egg Sauce.

Serves 4

Louise Gibbons

Tomato Sauce

1 medium onion, chopped
1 tablespoon margarine
salt and pepper to taste
1 (15-ounce) can diced tomatoes
6 sprigs mixed fresh herbs, such as thyme, oregano, basil,
   parsley and/or bay leaf

Add the onion to the heated margarine in a saucepan and sprinkle with salt and pepper. Sauté over low heat for 15 minutes, stirring occasionally. Add the tomatoes and herbs. Simmer for 20 minutes longer. Remove the herb sprigs and spoon into a serving bowl. Serve with a traditional codfish breakfast.

Serves 4   *Louise Gibbons*

Egg Sauce

2 tablespoons margarine
2 1/2 tablespoons flour
1 1/2 cups milk
3 hard-cooked eggs, finely chopped
salt and white pepper to taste

Melt the margarine in a saucepan over low heat. Stir in the flour gradually. Cook for 2 minutes, stirring constantly. Whisk in the milk until smooth. Cook until smooth, stirring constantly. Fold in the eggs and season with salt and white pepper. Serve with a traditional codfish breakfast.

Serves 4   *Louise Gibbons*

SMOOTH SAUCES

For sauces that develop lumps, use a metal whisk to beat out the lumps. Adding warmed milk or stock to the roux will help prevent lumps, as will using a thin roux.

North Shore Fish Cakes

and Eggs Benedict

FISH CAKES

1 pound salted codfish
12 ounces potatoes, peeled and cut into quarters
1/4 cup (1/2 stick) butter
1/2 medium onion, finely chopped
2 ribs celery, finely chopped
1 tablespoon finely chopped fresh parsley
1 1/2 teaspoons finely chopped fresh thyme
1 egg yolk
salt and pepper to taste
bread crumbs
vegetable oil for frying

For the fish cakes, soak the codfish in enough water to cover in a bowl for up to 3 days, changing the water at least 3 times; drain. Combine with the potatoes and enough fresh water to cover in a medium saucepan. Bring to a boil over medium heat and cook until the potatoes are tender. Drain and remove to a bowl; cover with a towel.

Melt the butter in a skillet. Add the onion and celery and sauté for 7 to 10 minutes or until the onion is translucent. Add to the codfish mixture and sprinkle with the parsley and thyme; mix well. Stir in the egg yolk and season with salt and pepper.

EGGS BENEDICT

12 to 14 eggs
6 or 7 cinnamon raisin English muffins, split and toasted
Curried Hollandaise Sauce (page 89)

Use a large spoon to shape the codfish mixture into 3- or 4-ounce patties. Roll in bread crumbs, coating evenly. Heat a skillet and coat with vegetable oil. Add to the skillet and fry for 5 minutes on each side or until golden brown and heated through.

For the eggs Benedict, bring a saucepan of water to a boil and reduce the heat. Crack each egg into a large spoon or ladle and slide gently into the water. Cook for 3 minutes. Remove gently with a slotted spoon.

Place 1 English muffin half on each serving plate and top with a fish cake and poached egg. Spoon Curried Hollandaise Sauce over the top. Serve immediately.

Serves 12 to 14

Danika Pereira,
Executive Chef to
His Excellency the Governor

Curried Hollandaise Sauce

1 small shallot, finely chopped
1 teaspoon curry powder
$^{1}/_{2}$ teaspoon ground coriander
$^{1}/_{2}$ teaspoon cumin
$^{1}/_{2}$ teaspoon turmeric
1 tablespoon lime juice
3 egg yolks
1 cup (2 sticks) butter, melted
salt and pepper to taste

Fill a medium saucepan halfway with water and bring to a boil; reduce the heat to a simmer.

Sauté the shallot in a small nonstick skillet for 3 to 5 minutes or until translucent; remove from the heat. Stir in the curry powder, coriander, cumin and turmeric. Sauté over low heat for 1 minute longer.

Combine the shallot mixture with the lime juice and egg yolks in a bowl and mix well. Place the bowl over the simmering water. Cook for 10 minutes or until frothy, whisking constantly. Remove from the saucepan of water.

Add the butter very gradually, whisking constantly until all the butter is incorporated and the mixture is smooth. You may whisk in water 1 teaspoon at a time if necessary for the desired consistency. Season with salt and pepper.

Serves 12 to 14

Danika Pereira,
Executive Chef to
His Excellency the Governor

BAIN-MARIE

A bain-marie, also known as a double boiler, is a shallow hot water bath in which another container is placed for slow and even heating. It is commonly used for melting chocolate and maintaining the delicate temperature of sauces.

Greek Quiche

1 unbaked (1-crust) refrigerator pie pastry
3 eggs, lightly beaten
1 cup milk
1/4 cup (1/2 stick) butter, melted
2 tablespoons flour
2 tablespoons grated Romano cheese

nutmeg to taste
1/4 teaspoon salt
1/4 teaspoon white pepper
1 (10-ounce) package frozen chopped spinach, thawed and drained
2 cups (8 ounces) crumbled feta cheese

Fit the pastry into a greased and floured 9-inch quiche pan. Trim and flute the edge and prick the bottom and side with a fork. Bake at 400 degrees for 3 minutes. Remove from the oven and gently prick again. Bake for 5 minutes longer. Reduce the oven temperature to 350 degrees.

Combine the eggs, milk, butter, flour, Romano cheese, nutmeg, salt and white pepper in a medium bowl; whisk to mix well. Fold in the spinach and feta cheese. Pour into the prepared pie shell.

Bake at 350 degrees for 35 minutes or until the filling is set and the pastry is golden brown. Let stand for 10 minutes before serving. Serve warm or at room temperature.

Serves 6

Beth Lindgren

Crustless Carrot Quiche

2 cups grated carrots
4 eggs
1 cup skim milk
1 small onion, chopped
1/2 teaspoon salt
1/2 teaspoon pepper
1 cup (4 ounces) shredded cheese

Combine the carrots with 1 inch cold water in a saucepan and bring to a boil. Cover and remove from the heat. Let stand for 5 minutes; drain well.

Combine the eggs, skim milk, onion, salt and pepper in a bowl and mix well. Stir in the carrots and cheese. Spoon into a 9-inch quiche dish sprayed with nonstick cooking spray.

Place the quiche dish in a larger baking pan and place on the oven rack. Add hot water to within 1/2 inch of the top of the quiche dish. Bake at 350 degrees for 35 to 40 minutes or until a knife inserted into the center comes out clean.

Serves 6   Barbara Cooper

MINT SUN TEA

For delicious iced tea, combine 2 tea bags, 1 quartered lemon, 1 handful fresh mint, 8 cups water and sugar to taste in a large container. Cover the container and place in the sun for 8 hours. Remove the tea bags and stir to dissolve the sugar completely. Chill until serving time.

Post-Marathon Frittata

1 tablespoon vegetable oil
1 pound chorizo or sweet Italian sausage, casing removed
1 orange bell pepper, chopped
1 yellow bell pepper, chopped
2 cups sliced fresh mushrooms
8 eggs
1/4 cup milk
1 cup (4 ounces) shredded Cheddar chese
salt and pepper to taste
parsley

Heat the oil in a heavy ovenproof 10-inch skillet. Add the sausage, bell peppers and mushrooms and sauté until the sausage is brown; drain. Whisk the eggs and milk together in a bowl. Pour over the sausage mixture and stir in the cheese, salt and pepper.

Place in a 350-degree oven and bake, covered, for 30 minutes. Remove the cover and bake for 10 minutes longer. Slice into wedges to serve. Garnish with parsley and serve warm.

Variations: You can include almost any savoury item in a frittata, as long as it is precooked or can be eaten uncooked. Meat, vegetables, pasta and many varieties of cheese are all excellent ingredients to include in a frittata. Leftovers are great for the next day's breakfast or lunch.

Serves 8

Christa Cooper

PLAYING CARDS *Our Bermuda-themed playing card fund-raiser was the brainchild of our founder, Mrs. C. Vail Zuill. Launched in 1994, our first installment of 5,000 sets sold out within 18 months. These continue to sell successfully island-wide.*

Yoghurt and Fruit Parfaits

STONE FRUIT PARFAIT

2 peaches
2 nectarines
4 apricots
4 plums
1 cup sugar
1 cup cranberry juice
1 vanilla bean
1 cinnamon stick
16 ounces plain yoghurt

TROPICAL FRUIT PARFAIT

1 cup chopped mixed mango, pineapple,
    guava and kiwifruit
16 ounces passion fruit yoghurt

MIXED BERRY PARFAIT

1 cup mixed berries
16 ounces strawberry yoghurt

For the stone fruit parfait, peel the peaches, nectarines, apricots and plums and cut into small pieces, discarding the seeds. Combine the fruit with the sugar, cranberry juice, vanilla bean and cinnamon stick in a saucepan and mix well.

Bring to a boil over medium heat. Reduce the heat and simmer for 10 to 15 minutes or until the fruit is tender. Let stand until cool and chill in the refrigerator; discard the vanilla bean and cinnamon stick.

Alternate layers of the fruit mixture and plain yoghurt in Champagne glasses until all the ingredients are used. Chill until serving time.

For the tropical fruit parfait, layer the fresh mango, pineapple, guava and kiwifruit with the passion fruit yoghurt in Champagne glasses. Chill until serving time.

For the mixed berry parfait, layer the mixed berries with the strawberry yoghurt in Champagne glasses. Chill until serving time.

Serves 4 to 6

Danika Pereira,
Executive Chef to
His Excellency
the Governor

Banana Fritters

2 cups flour
3 tablespoons sugar
2 tablespoons baking powder
1¹/₂ cups milk
¹/₄ cup (¹/₂ stick) butter, melted

1 egg
1 teaspoon dark rum
1 teaspoon nut liqueur
3 large bananas, mashed
Macadamia Syrup (page 95)

Combine the flour, sugar and baking powder in a bowl. Add the milk, butter, egg, rum and liqueur and mix until smooth. Stir in the mashed bananas.

Spray a griddle with nonstick cooking spray and heat. Spoon the batter into 3-inch fritters on the heated griddle and cook for 2 minutes. Turn the fritters and cook until golden brown. Serve with the Macadamia Syrup.

Serves 6 to 8

Danika Pereira,
Executive Chef to His Excellency the Governor

Macadamia Syrup

4 ounces chopped macadamias
12 ounces maple syrup

Spread the macadamias in a baking pan. Toast at 350 degrees for 10 minutes or until golden brown. Combine with the syrup in a pitcher. Let stand to infuse flavours. Serve with Banana Fritters or Sunday Morning Pancakes.

Serves 6 to 8

Danika Pereira,
Executive Chef to
His Excellency the Governor

Sunday Morning Pancakes

2 egg whites
2 cups flour
4 teaspoons baking powder
2 tablespoons sugar
$1/2$ teaspoon salt
2 egg yolks
$1^3/4$ cups milk
$1/2$ cup (1 stick) butter, melted

Beat the egg whites in a bowl until stiff peaks form. Mix the flour, baking powder, sugar and salt in a mixing bowl. Add the egg yolks, milk and butter gradually, mixing until smooth. Beat in the egg whites at low speed.

Heat a nonstick griddle over medium-high heat. Pour the batter by $1/4$ cupfuls onto the griddle. Cook until bubbles appear on the surface. Turn the pancakes and cook until golden brown. Serve hot with syrup.

Serves 6

Tegan Smith

CHOCOLATE MOCHA SHAKE

For a brunch pick-me-up, combine 1/2 cup chilled espresso coffee and 4 ounces semisweet chocolate in a blender. Add 4 scoops ice cream and blend until smooth. Add milk and sugar for the desired consistency and degree of sweetness. Pour into coffee mugs and garnish with whipped cream and chocolate curls.

Apple French Toast

ORANGE JULIUS

Orange Julius is a delicious and refreshing breakfast drink. Mix ½ cup sugar, 1 cup cold water, 1 cup milk, one 6-ounce can frozen orange juice concentrate, 1 egg and 1 teaspoon vanilla extract in a blender. Add 16 ice cubes and process until smooth. Serve over ice. You can also add bananas and strawberries to vary the flavour.

1 thin baguette
3 large Granny Smith apples
5 tablespoons butter
1 cup packed brown sugar
2 tablespoons corn syrup
1 teaspoon cinnamon
3 eggs
1 cup milk
1 teaspoon vanilla extract

Cut the baguette into 1-inch slices. Peel the apples and cut each apple into 16 wedges, discarding the cores. Melt the butter in a large skillet. Add the apples and cook just until the apples are tender. Add the brown sugar, corn syrup and cinnamon. Cook over low heat until the apples are caramelised, stirring constantly. Spoon into a buttered 9×13-inch baking dish.

Cover the apple mixture with a single layer of bread slices. Mix the eggs, milk and vanilla in a bowl. Pour over the bread. Cover with plastic wrap and chill in the refrigerator for 8 hours or longer. Bake at 375 degrees for 30 minutes.

Serves 6

Beth Lindgren

Sunrise Cobbler

5 cups sliced fresh peaches
1¼ cups fresh or frozen raspberries
½ cup packed brown sugar
1 tablespoon cornstarch
¾ cup oats
¾ cup flour
¼ cup sugar
2 teaspoons baking powder
¾ cup buttermilk

Mix the peaches and raspberries with the brown sugar and cornstarch in a large bowl. Spoon into a 2-quart baking dish sprayed with nonstick cooking spray.

Combine the oats, flour, sugar, baking powder and buttermilk in a medium bowl and mix well. Drop over the fruit in 8 or 10 mounds. Bake at 375 degrees for 35 to 40 minutes or until the topping is golden brown.

Serves 6   *Elizabeth Zalinger*

SHERBET PUNCH

Punch made with sherbet is easy to serve at brunch. Combine 1 gallon softened lemon sherbet or lime sherbet with 1 bottle of inexpensive champagne in a large punch bowl and mix gently. Add several slices of lemon or lime and serve immediately.

Cinnamon Walnut Coffee Cake

**CARIBBEAN
ICED COFFEE**

To create a coffee with an island flavour to go with coffee cake, mix strong coffee with sweetened cream of coconut to taste. Chill until serving time and serve over ice with a splash of rum.

COFFEE CAKE

2 cups flour
1 teaspoon baking powder
1 teaspoon baking soda
1/4 teaspoon salt
1/2 cup (1 stick) margarine
   or butter, softened
1 cup sugar
2 eggs
1 cup sour cream
1 teaspoon vanilla extract
1/4 cup packed brown sugar
1 teaspoon cinnamon
1/2 cup chopped walnuts

LEMON GLAZE

1/2 cup icing sugar
1 teaspoon milk
2 teaspoons lemon juice

For the coffee cake, mix the flour, baking powder, baking soda and salt together. Cream the margarine and sugar in a mixing bowl until light and fluffy. Beat in the eggs 1 at a time. Add the sour cream and vanilla and mix well. Add the dry ingredients and beat until smooth. Spread half the batter in a greased and floured tube pan or bundt pan.

Combine the brown sugar, cinnamon and walnuts in a bowl and mix well. Sprinkle half the mixture in the prepared tube pan. Spread the remaining batter over the walnut mixture and top with the remaining walnut mixture.

Bake at 350 degrees for 25 to 30 minutes or until a wooden pick inserted near the center comes out clean. Cool in the pan for 10 minutes and remove to a wire rack to cool completely. Place on a serving plate.

For the glaze, combine the icing sugar, milk and lemon juice in a bowl and mix until smooth. Drizzle over the coffee cake.

You can substitute an equal amount of sugar mixed with 1/4 cup light or dark molasses for every cup of brown sugar any time you are out of brown sugar.

Serves 12

Wendy Railton

Cheddar Bacon Muffins

10 slices bacon, chopped
1 egg
1 cup milk
1³/₄ cups flour
2 tablespoons sugar
1 teaspoon baking powder
1 teaspoon salt
1¹/₂ cups (6 ounces) shredded Cheddar cheese
3 tablespoons butter, melted

Fry the bacon in a skillet until crisp. Remove to paper towels to drain and reserve 2 tablespoons of the drippings. Combine the reserved drippings with the egg and milk in a bowl and mix well.

Mix the flour, sugar, baking powder and salt in a bowl. Stir in the cheese and bacon. Add the egg mixture and mix just until moistened.

Spoon the mixture into lightly greased muffin cups. Brush with the melted butter. Bake at 400 degrees for 20 to 25 minutes or until golden brown.

Makes 1 dozen

Kim Moseley

BAKING POWDER

To test whether baking powder has lost it oomph, stir ¹/₂ teaspoon into a glass of warm water. If it foams to the top, the baking powder is still active.

Cranberry Orange Oat Muffins

1$\frac{1}{3}$ cups flour
$\frac{3}{4}$ cup quick-cooking oats
$\frac{3}{4}$ cup sugar
2 teaspoons baking powder
$\frac{1}{2}$ teaspoon baking soda
$\frac{1}{2}$ teaspoon cinnamon
$\frac{1}{4}$ teaspoon salt
$\frac{3}{4}$ cup milk
3 tablespoons vegetable oil
1 egg, beaten
$\frac{3}{4}$ cup chopped fresh cranberries
2 tablespoons grated orange zest

Mix the flour, oats, sugar, baking powder, baking soda, cinnamon and salt in a bowl. Make a well in the center. Place the milk, oil, egg, cranberries and orange zest in the well and mix just until moistened.

Spoon into 12 greased or paper-lined muffin cups, filling $\frac{2}{3}$ full. Bake at 450 degrees for 18 to 20 minutes or until the tops are light brown. Cool in the pan for 10 minutes and remove to a wire rack to cool completely.

Makes 1 dozen

Diane Steiger

Zucchini Muffins

1 cup all-purpose flour
1 cup whole wheat flour
1 teaspoon baking powder
nutmeg to taste
$^1/_2$ teaspoon salt
$^3/_4$ cup sugar
2 eggs
$^1/_4$ cup vegetable oil
$^1/_4$ cup unsweetened applesauce
1$^1/_2$ cups peeled and grated zucchini
$^1/_2$ cup raisins

Sift the all-purpose flour, whole wheat flour, baking powder, nutmeg and salt together. Combine the sugar, eggs, oil and applesauce in a large mixing bowl and mix for 1 minute. Add the dry ingredients and mix well. Add the zucchini and raisins and mix just until moistened.

Spoon into 12 greased or paper-lined muffin cups, filling $^2/_3$ full. Bake at 350 degrees for 15 minutes or until the tops are golden brown and a wooden pick inserted into the center comes out clean. Cool in the pan for 5 minutes and remove to a wire rack to cool completely.

Makes 1 dozen

Louise Gibbons

Banana Bread

with Rum and Golden Raisins

RASPBERRY CAPPUCCINO

You can create a delicious variation on cappuccino at home. Blend 1 1/2 cups chocolate milk, 2/3 cup chilled espresso and 1/4 cup chocolate syrup in a blender. Add 3 cups coffee ice cream and 2 cups frozen fresh raspberries. Process until smooth. Pour into 4 glasses. Rinse the blender and add 1 cup cold milk. Process at high speed for 20 seconds or until the milk is frothy. Add to the chocolate mixture and garnish with chocolate curls.

4 ounces golden raisins
1/3 cup dark rum
1 1/2 cups flour
2 teaspoons baking powder
1/2 teaspoon baking soda
1/2 teaspoon salt
1/2 cup (1 stick) unsalted butter, melted
2/3 cup sugar
2 eggs
4 small ripe bananas, mashed
3/4 cup chopped walnuts
1 teaspoon vanilla extract

Combine the raisins and rum in a saucepan and bring to a boil. Remove from the heat and let stand for 1 hour.

Mix the flour, baking powder, baking soda and salt in a medium bowl. Combine the melted butter and sugar in a large bowl and mix well. Beat in the eggs 1 at a time. Add the bananas, walnuts, vanilla and raisins. Stir in the dry ingredients.

Spoon into a loaf pan lined with baking parchment. Bake at 350 degrees for 1 to 1 1/4 hours or until the bread tests done. Cool in the pan for 10 minutes and remove to a wire rack to cool completely.

Serves 12

Mary Mello

Bermuda Banana Bread

1^{1}/$_{2}$ cups sifted whole wheat flour
1 teaspoon baking powder
1 teaspoon baking soda
1 teaspoon salt
^{1}/$_{2}$ cup canola oil
2 eggs

1^{1}/$_{2}$ cups mashed ripe bananas
^{1}/$_{2}$ cup packed brown sugar
1 teaspoon ginger
^{1}/$_{2}$ teaspoon cinnamon
1 tablespoon grated lemon zest

Mix the whole wheat flour, baking powder, baking soda and salt in a large bowl. Combine the canola oil, eggs and bananas in a mixing bowl and beat until smooth. Add the brown sugar, ginger, cinnamon and lemon zest and mix well. Fold gently into the dry ingredients, mixing just until moistened.

Spoon into an oiled and floured loaf pan. Bake at 350 degrees for 50 to 60 minutes or until the bread tests done. Cool in the pan for 10 minutes and remove to a wire rack to cool completely.

You can crush the juice from fresh gingerroot to substitute for the ground ginger if preferred.

Serves 12

Antoine Hunt

Basic Scones

3 cups unbleached flour
3 tablespoons sugar
2 1/2 teaspoons baking powder
1/2 teaspoon baking soda

1/2 teaspoon salt
1/2 cup (1 stick) plus 2 tablespoons cold unsalted
  butter, chopped
1 cup cold buttermilk

Mix the flour, sugar, baking powder, baking soda and salt together in a bowl. Cut in the butter with a pastry blender until the mixture resembles coarse crumbs. Add the buttermilk and stir to form a sticky dough. Knead the dough gently on a lightly floured surface just until the mixture is smooth; do not overwork the dough. Pat into a circle 3/4 inch thick and cut into wedges or circles.

Place on a baking sheet lined with baking parchment. Bake at 400 degrees for 14 to 18 minutes or until golden brown. Cool slightly on a wire rack. Serve with fruit jam and clotted cream or whipped heavy cream.

For *Fruit and Spice Scones,* add 1 teaspoon cardamom and 1 cup chopped apricots or 2 teaspoons grated fresh orange zest and 1 cup dried cranberries.

Serves 12

Danika Pereira,
Executive Chef to His Excellency the Governor

Eggnog Bread

3 cups flour
1 cup sugar
1 tablespoon baking powder
$1/2$ teaspoon nutmeg
$1/2$ teaspoon cinnamon
1 teaspoon salt
$1^{1}/2$ cups eggnog
1 egg, beaten
$1/4$ cup ($1/2$ stick) butter, melted
$3/4$ cup chopped candied fruit
1 cup pecans

Sift the flour, sugar, baking powder, nutmeg, cinnamon and salt into a bowl. Mix the eggnog, egg and butter in a small bowl. Add to the flour mixture and mix until smooth. Stir in the candied fruit and pecans.

Spoon into a lightly greased loaf pan. Bake at 350 degrees for 1 hour. Cool in the pan for 10 minutes and remove to a wire rack to cool completely.

Serves 12

Kathy Suter

CHRISTMAS CARDS *Each year, the BJSL sells unique Bermuda-themed christmas cards designed by local resident artists. More than 50,000 cards are sold each year.*

Johnny Bread

5 cups flour
1¹/₂ cups sugar
7 teaspoons baking powder
1¹/₂ teaspoons salt
1 cup skim milk
1 cup (2 sticks) margarine, melted
4 eggs, beaten
¹/₄ cup vegetable oil

Mix the flour, sugar, baking powder and salt in a large bowl. Add the milk, margarine and eggs and mix by hand until moistened. Shape into a flattened 9-inch round loaf.

Heat the oil in a large skillet or griddle. Add the bread and cook for about 20 minutes or until brown on both sides, turning once.

Makes 1 loaf

Kendra Wharton

Pumpkin Nut Bread

3^1/$_3$ cups flour
^{1}/$_2$ teaspoon baking powder
2 teaspoons baking soda
1 teaspoon cinnamon
^{1}/$_2$ teaspoon nutmeg
^{1}/$_2$ teaspoon ground cloves
1^1/$_2$ teaspoons salt
^{2}/$_3$ cup shortening
2 cups mashed cooked pumpkin
4 eggs
2^2/$_3$ cups sugar
^{2}/$_3$ cup milk
1 cup chopped walnuts

Whisk the flour, baking powder, baking soda, cinnamon, nutmeg, cloves and salt together in a bowl. Combine the shortening, pumpkin, eggs, sugar, milk and walnuts in a large mixing bowl and mix well. Add the dry ingredients and mix just until moistened; small lumps of shortening may remain.

Spoon into 2 greased and floured large loaf pans. Bake at 350 degrees or until a wooden pick inserted into the center comes out clean. Cool in the pans for 5 minutes and remove to a wire rack to cool completely.

Makes 2 loaves

Pamela Shaw

Hot Cross Buns

1 (1-tablespoon) package dry yeast
1 cup warm water
2¹/2 cups flour
2 tablespoons sugar
1 tablespoon cinnamon
¹/4 teaspoon nutmeg

pinch of salt
1 egg
¹/2 cup (1 stick) butter, softened
³/4 cup currants
2 egg whites, beaten, or ¹/4 cup egg white substitute
1 cup icing sugar

Dissolve the yeast in the warm water in a large bowl. Mix the flour, sugar, cinnamon, nutmeg and salt in a medium bowl. Add half the dry ingredients to the yeast mixture and beat until smooth. Beat in the egg and butter. Beat in the remaining dry ingredients with the currants.

Place in a greased bowl and brush the top with oil. Cover and let rise in a warm place for 30 minutes or until doubled in bulk. Stir down the dough and shape into 15 small balls. Place on a baking sheet with sides touching. Let rise, covered, in a warm place for 30 minutes.

Snip the top of each bun with scissors in the form of a cross. Brush with a mixture of the beaten egg whites and icing sugar. Bake at 400 degrees for 15 to 20 minutes or until golden brown.

Makes 15

Carolyn Toogood

Delicious Cinnamon Rolls

CINNAMON ROLLS

1 (1-tablespoon) package dry yeast
3/4 teaspoon salt
1/3 cup sugar
2 1/2 to 3 cups flour
1/2 cup milk
1/3 cup water
3 tablespoons butter
1 egg, beaten
1/2 cup sugar
1 teaspoon cinnamon
2 tablespoons butter, melted

CINNAMON ROLL FROSTING

1 cup icing sugar
2 teaspoons milk
1 teaspoon butter, softened

For the cinnamon rolls, mix the yeast and salt with 1/3 cup sugar and 1 cup of the flour in a small bowl. Combine the milk, water and 3 tablespoons butter in a saucepan and warm over low heat. Add the yeast mixture gradually, mixing constantly until smooth. Remove from the heat and add the egg and 1/2 cup flour; mix well. Mix in 1 cup flour until smooth.

Knead on a lightly floured surface until smooth, kneading in the remaining 1/2 cup flour if necessary. Place in a bowl sprayed with nonstick cooking spray and turn to coat the surface. Cover with plastic wrap and let rise for 20 minutes or longer.

Mix 1/2 cup sugar with the cinnamon in a bowl. Punch down the dough and roll into a large rectangle. Brush with the melted butter and sprinkle with the cinnamon-sugar. Roll up the dough from the long side and cut into 18 slices.

Place the slices cut side down 2 inches apart on a greased baking sheet or place in greased muffin cups. Bake at 375 degrees for 15 to 20 minutes or until golden brown. You may brush again with butter if desired.

For the frosting, blend the icing sugar with the milk and butter in a bowl. Spread over the cinnamon rolls.

Makes 1 1/2 dozen

Elizabeth Zalinger

Sweet White Bread or Rolls

1 cup sugar
1/4 cup shortening
4 teaspoons salt
2 cups boiling water
1 cup cold water
1 teaspoon sugar
1 cup lukewarm (105- to 115-degree) water
4 (1-tablespoon) packages dry yeast
9 1/2 cups flour
1 tablespoon butter, melted

Combine 1 cup sugar with the shortening and salt in a large bowl. Add the boiling water and stir until the sugar dissolves and the shortening melts. Add the cold water.

Combine 1 teaspoon sugar with the lukewarm water in a small bowl. Sprinkle the yeast into the water and let stand for 10 minutes. Stir into the shortening mixture. Add the flour and mix to form a dough. Knead on a floured surface until smooth and elastic. Shape into loaves or rolls. Place on lightly greased baking sheets and let rise for 1 hour.

Place in a 350-degree oven. Bake the loaves for 1 hour or the rolls for 45 minutes, brushing with the melted butter during the baking time.

Makes 3 or 4 large loaves or 3 to 4 dozen rolls

Melanie Whaley

TOY SHOP *In 1940, a restriction was placed on the importation of toys to Bermuda. The BJSL opened The BJSL Toy Shop, where they sold Bermudian handcrafted toys.*

Italian Sandwich

1 loaf round Italian bread
2 tablespoons olive oil
6 ounces goat cheese, crumbled
12 slices prosciutto
1/2 green bell pepper, roasted and sliced

1/2 yellow bell pepper, roasted and sliced
1/2 red bell pepper, roasted and sliced
1 large onion, sliced into rings and lightly roasted
12 fresh basil leaves, chopped

Cut the bread into halves horizontally and reserve the top half. Drizzle the cut side of the bottom with 1 tablespoon of the olive oil and the goat cheese. Layer the prosciutto, bell peppers, onion and basil over the goat cheese and drizzle with the remaining 1 tablespoon olive oil.

Replace the sandwich top and wrap tightly with plastic wrap. Chill in the refrigerator for up to 24 hours. Cut into wedges to serve.

Ham, mozzarella cheese, sun-dried tomatoes, olives, fresh herbs, spinach and arugula may also be used as alternative fillings for the sandwich.

Serves 6

Louise Gibbons

BREAD MAKEOVER

You can refresh slightly stale French bread in the oven. Place it in a brown paper bag, splash the bag with water, and place it in a low oven for 3 to 5 minutes or until the bread becomes soft again. Just remember to use a brown bag that does not contain recycled material and to watch the bread carefully as you heat it.

Cool Summer Sandwich

1/2 cup plain nonfat yoghurt
4 ounces nonfat cream cheese, softened
1 garlic clove, minced
1/2 teaspoon dried thyme
1/2 teaspoon dried rosemary
1/2 teaspoon dried chives
1/2 teaspoon dried basil
1 large French baguette
3 large ripe tomatoes, thinly sliced
1 medium Bermuda onion, thinly sliced

Line a colander with a large coffee filter or cheesecloth and add the yoghurt. Place over a large bowl and place in the refrigerator for 3 hours to drain. Combine the drained yoghurt with the cream cheese, garlic, thyme, rosemary, chives and basil in a medium bowl and mix well.

Cut the bread into halves horizontally. Spread the yoghurt mixture evenly over the bottom half. Layer the tomato and onion slices over the yoghurt mixture and replace the top of the bread.

Wrap tightly with plastic wrap and chill in the refrigerator for 20 minutes. Cut into 4 pieces to serve.

Serves 4

Elizabeth Zalinger

English Tea Sandwiches

4 slices white bread
4 slices whole wheat bread
softened butter
2 hard-cooked eggs, finely chopped
mayonnaise

1 English cucumber, peeled
smoked salmon
shredded Cheddar cheese
English watercress or alfalfa sprouts

Cut the crusts from the bread and spread the slices thinly with butter. Spread 1 of the fillings over half the bread slices and top with the remaining slices. Cut each sandwich into 3 fingers.

For an egg tea sandwich, combine the egg with enough mayonnaise to bind in a bowl. Proceed as above using white bread.

For a cucumber tea sandwich, slice the English cucumber very thin and proceed as above using white bread.

For a smoked salmon tea sandwich, slice the English cucumber and smoked salmon very thin and proceed as above using whole wheat bread.

For a watercress sandwich, proceed as above, sprinkling whole wheat bread with shredded Cheddar cheese and English watercress.

Makes 12 finger sandwiches

Louise Gibbons

Bermuda Fried Fish Sandwiches

TARTAR SAUCE

1/4 cup mayonnaise
1 teaspoon mustard
1 teaspoon sweet pickle relish
1 dill pickle, chopped
2 tablespoons finely chopped Bermuda onion

FISH SANDWICHES

1 egg
1 1/2 cups evaporated milk
3 pounds Bermuda snapper fillets, wahoo fillets
   or bonita fillets
3 tablespoons (or more) paprika
seasoning salt and pepper to taste
1 cup each flour and crushed cornflakes
corn oil for frying
12 slices raisin bread
shredded cheese, coleslaw, lettuce and/or
   sliced tomatoes

For the tartar sauce, blend the mayonnaise with the mustard in a bowl. Add the pickle relish, dill pickle and onion and mix well. Chill until serving time.

For the sandwiches, beat the egg with the evaporated milk in a bowl. Add the fish and marinate in the refrigerator for 2 hours or longer; drain. Mix the paprika, seasoning salt and pepper together. Mix the crushed cornflakes with the flour in a bowl. Sprinkle the fish with the seasoning mixture and coat with the cornflake mixture. Heat 1/2 inch corn oil in a heavy skillet or deep fryer. Add the fish and fry until golden brown on both sides. Remove to a paper towel to drain.

Serve on the raisin bread with the tartar sauce and a choice of cheese, coleslaw, lettuce and tomato. You may also serve the fish with the tartar sauce, hot sauce and lemon wedges.

Serves 6   *Tammy Gibbons*

Open-Face Crab Melt

1/2 cup (1 stick) butter, softened
1 1/2 teaspoons mayonnaise
1/4 teaspoon garlic powder
1/4 teaspoon seasoning salt
2 (6-ounce) cans crab meat, drained and flaked
1 (5-ounce) jar Old English sharp cheese spread
6 English muffins

Blend the butter and mayonnaise with the garlic powder and seasoning salt in a bowl. Add the crab meat and cheese and mix well.

Split the English muffins into halves horizontally. Spread with the crab meat mixture and arrange on a baking sheet. Bake at 350 degrees for 10 to 12 minutes or until bubbly.

Serves 6   *Amy Stone*

COIN DRIVE *This important fund-raiser invites the public to donate their loose change in buckets located in prominent places around the island.*

Soups & Salads

Caldo Verde

2 tablespoons olive oil
1/2 cup minced onion
2 teaspoons minced garlic
2 pounds red potatoes, peeled and sliced
2 quarts (8 cups) water

Tabasco sauce to taste
salt and pepper to taste
12 ounces chorizo or garlic sausage, chopped
1 pound kale or mustard greens, trimmed

Heat the olive oil in a saucepan and add the onion. Sauté for 2 minutes. Add the garlic and sauté for 2 minutes longer. Add the potatoes, water, Tabasco sauce, salt and pepper. Bring to a boil and reduce the heat. Simmer for 15 minutes or until the potatoes are tender. Process the mixture in batches in a food processor. Combine the batches in the saucepan.

Sauté the sausage in a skillet; drain and add to the saucepan. Simmer for 5 minutes.

Adjust the seasonings. Stir in the kale. Simmer for 5 minutes, stirring frequently. Ladle into soup bowls and serve hot.

Serves 8

Joe Gibbons

Carrot Soup

2 bunches carrots, peeled and sliced
bulbs and 2 inches of the green tops of
   6 to 8 green onions

3 (10-ounce) cans chicken broth
2/3 cup sweet mango chutney
2 cups half-and-half

Combine the carrots, green onions and chicken broth in a saucepan and cook until the carrots are tender; drain, reserving the broth. Combine the carrot mixture with the mango chutney in a food processor and process until smooth. Return to the broth in the saucepan and add the half-and-half. Heat just to serving temperature; do not boil. Ladle into soup bowls.

You may also cool the soup base and then stir in the half-and-half. Chill until serving time and serve cold.

Serves 8

Pam Kempe

Split Green Pea Soup

2 cups dried split green peas
2 tablespoons butter
1/2 cup chopped Bermuda onion
1/2 cup thinly sliced carrots
1 ham hock
1 bay leaf
6 sprigs of fresh thyme
1 chicken bouillon cube
dark rum to taste
1/2 teaspoon salt
1/8 teaspoon pepper
chopped fresh parsley or chives (optional)

Combine the dried peas with enough water to cover in a heavy 3-quart saucepan and bring to a boil. Reduce the heat and simmer for 5 minutes. Let stand, covered, for 1 1/2 to 2 hours, adding additional water if necessary to cover the peas.

Melt the butter in a medium saucepan. Add the onion and sauté until barely translucent. Add the carrots and sauté for 2 minutes.

Return the peas to a boil and add the ham hock, bay leaf and thyme. Reduce the heat and simmer, covered, for 2 to 2 1/2 hours or until the peas are tender, stirring frequently. Add the bouillon cube and stir to dissolve completely.

Remove the ham hock and cut the meat from the bone. Remove and discard the bay leaf. Let the peas stand until cool. Add the onion and carrot mixture, the ham and the rum to the soup. Reheat the soup to serving temperature and season with the salt and pepper. Ladle into soup bowls and sprinkle with parsley or chives.

Serves 6

Carolyn Toogood

Roasted Red Pepper Soup

SOUP FIRST AID

If your soup is too salty or spicy, add an uncooked potato and cook a while longer. You can remove the potato before serving, and it will also serve to thicken the soup. As an alternative for cream-based soups, you can add additional cream.

3 red bell peppers
3/4 cup olive oil
1 1/2 cups chopped onions
2 tablespoons chopped garlic
4 teaspoons fennel seeds
1 teaspoon thyme
2 bay leaves
4 teaspoons basil
1 jalapeño chile
2 (16-ounce) cans diced tomatoes
4 (10-ounce) cans chicken broth
1 (6-ounce) can tomato paste
1 cup heavy cream
4 cups half-and-half
salt and pepper to taste

Cut off the stem ends of the bell peppers and discard the seeds. Place the peppers directly on the burner of a gas grill and grill until charred, turning to char evenly. Place in a plastic bag and let stand for 10 to 15 minutes. Wash off the skins and reserve the peppers.

Heat the olive oil in a saucepan and add the onions, garlic, fennel seeds, thyme, bay leaves, basil and jalapeño chile. Sauté for 10 minutes or until the onions are tender. Combine with the reserved bell peppers, tomatoes, chicken broth and half the tomato paste in the saucepan and mix well. Process in several batches in a food processor or blender until smooth. Combine the batches in the saucepan and add the remaining tomato paste, cream and half-and-half. Season with salt and pepper. Simmer for 30 minutes. Strain into another saucepan and ladle into soup bowls. Serve as a first course for steak, fish or pork.

Serves 8

Wendi Ryland

Curried Pumpkin Soup

1/2 cup chopped onion
2 tablespoons butter or margarine
2 cups chicken stock or vegetable stock
1 large potato, chopped
1 teaspoon curry powder, or to taste

1/8 teaspoon thyme
1/2 teaspoon salt
1/4 teaspoon pepper
2 cups canned pumpkin or mashed cooked pumpkin
2 cups (or more) milk

Sauté the onion in the butter in a large saucepan until tender but not brown. Add the chicken stock, potato, curry powder, thyme, salt and pepper. Simmer until the potato is tender. Process the mixture in a blender and return to the saucepan.

Add the pumpkin and milk and mix well. Simmer until heated through, adding more milk if necessary for the desired consistency. Adjust the seasonings and ladle into soup bowls.

Serves 6

Susan Smith

Butternut Squash and Apple Soup

1 medium onion, chopped
1 fennel bulb, chopped
3 ribs celery, chopped
1/2 cup (1 stick) butter
5 pounds butternut squash, peeled and chopped
4 cups (1 quart) chicken bouillon or
   vegetable bouillon

3 apples, peeled and chopped
1 cup heavy cream, or to taste
nutmeg, salt and white pepper to taste
fennel greens
toasted pumpkin seeds, or cranberries simmered
   in a light syrup

Sauté the onion, fennel and celery in the butter in a saucepan until tender. Add the squash, apples and chicken bouillon and cook until the squash and apples are tender. Process the mixture in a blender until smooth.

Strain back into the saucepan. Add the cream and season with nutmeg, salt and white pepper. Simmer just until heated through. Ladle into soup bowls and top with fennel greens. You may garnish with toasted pumpkin seeds or cranberries simmered in a light syrup if desired.

You may omit the cream for a lighter version of this soup.

Serves 4

Frantz Wolmuth,
Executive Chef, Bank of Bermuda

Cold Avocado Soup

3 large very ripe avocados, chopped
1/4 cup chopped onion
1 cup light cream or buttermilk
1 (10-ounce) can cream of chicken soup
1/2 teaspoon seasoned salt
chopped chives

Combine the avocados with the onion, cream, cream of chicken soup and seasoned salt in a blender. Process until smooth. Chill until serving time. Ladle into soup bowls and top with chopped chives.

Serves 6

Susan Smith

Tomato Dill Bisque

4 large tomatoes, peeled
2 medium onions, chopped
2 garlic cloves, chopped
2 tablespoons margarine
1 cube chicken bouillon
1/2 cup water

3/4 teaspoon dried dill weed, or 2 1/2 teaspoons
  chopped fresh dill weed
1/4 teaspoon salt
1/8 teaspoon pepper
1/2 cup mayonnaise

Chop the tomatoes into a large bowl and reserve 1/4 cup of the accumulated tomato juice, pressing the tomatoes if necessary to produce juice. Sauté the onions and garlic in the margarine in a saucepan for 3 minutes. Add the tomatoes, chicken bouillon, water, dill weed, salt and pepper and mix well. Simmer, covered, for 10 minutes. Let stand until cool.

Process 1/2 at a time in a blender until smooth. Combine the mixtures in a bowl. Mix the reserved tomato juice and the mayonnaise in a cup and add to the bisque; mix well. Chill until serving time. Serve cold.

You may substitute one 28-ounce can of whole tomatoes for the fresh tomatoes in this recipe and reduce the cooking time accordingly. This soup is best made 1 day before serving.

Serves 4

Cornelia Kempe

Chilled Cucumber Soup

1 cucumber, peeled
8 ounces potato, chopped and cooked
5 ounces plain yoghurt
2 ounces cream cheese, softened
2 cups milk
1 tablespoon vinegar
salt and pepper to taste

Cut 3 thin slices from the cucumber for garnish. Chop the remaining cucumber and combine with the potato, yoghurt, cream cheese, milk, vinegar, salt and pepper in a blender. Process until smooth and adjust the seasonings. Chill for 2 to 3 hours. Ladle into soup bowls and top with the reserved cucumber slices.

Serves 6

Susan Ternent

Pasta and Bean Soup

CHEESE RIND

Freeze the rind of aged Parmesan cheese and use it to flavour vegetable soups as they cook. Discard the rind before serving the soup.

2 teaspoons canola oil
$1/2$ cup chopped onion
$1/3$ cup chopped carrot
$1/3$ cup chopped celery
2 teaspoons crushed garlic
2 cups canned tomatoes, crushed
$3^{1/2}$ cups nonfat chicken stock
1 teaspoon dried basil
$1/2$ teaspoon dried oregano
1 (14-ounce) can red kidney beans, drained
1 (14-ounce) can white kidney beans, drained
$2/3$ cup uncooked macaroni
3 tablespoons grated Parmesan cheese

Heat the canola oil in a large nonstick saucepan sprayed with nonstick vegetable oil. Add the onion, carrot, celery and garlic and sauté for 5 minutes. Add the tomatoes, chicken stock, basil and oregano and mix well.

Spoon $2/3$ of the red beans and $2/3$ of the white beans into the saucepan. Mash the remaining beans and add to the soup. Simmer for 15 minutes, stirring occasionally. Stir in the pasta and simmer for 5 to 8 minutes or until the pasta is tender. Ladle into soup bowls and sprinkle with the Parmesan cheese.

Serves 4   *Melanie Holmes*

Slow-Cooker Brunswick Stew

1 (16-ounce) can diced tomatoes
1 (6-ounce) can tomato paste
3 cups chopped cooked chicken
1 (10-ounce) package frozen succotash, or frozen sliced okra
1 cup chopped onion
1 bay leaf
1/2 teaspoon dried rosemary, crushed
ground cloves to taste
1 teaspoon salt
1/2 teaspoon pepper
2 1/2 cups chicken stock

Mix the undrained tomatoes and tomato paste in a slow cooker. Add the chicken, succotash, onion, bay leaf, rosemary, cloves, salt and pepper. Stir in the chicken stock.

Cook, covered, on Low for 5 to 6 hours or until done to taste. Discard the bay leaf and stir to mix well before serving.

Serves 6

Kim Paterson

DON'T LEAVE YOUR DRINK *BJSL developed and implemented a campaign to promote awareness of the potential for unguarded drinks to be spiked with drugs.*

Italian Meatball Soup

MEATBALLS

12 ounces ground beef
1/3 cup seasoned bread crumbs
1 egg, lightly beaten
2 tablespoons grated Parmesan cheese
2 tablespoons finely chopped parsley
1/4 teaspoon pepper
2 tablespoons olive oil

SOUP

1 cup chopped onion
2 tablespoons butter
1 (10-ounce) can beef broth
1 cup water
2 (15-ounce) cans whole peeled tomatoes
1 teaspoon dried oregano
1/2 teaspoon sugar
1 (10-ounce) package frozen green beans, partially
   thawed
1/2 cup uncooked ditalini
grated Parmesan cheese

For the meatballs, combine the ground beef, bread crumbs, egg, Parmesan cheese, parsley and pepper in a bowl. Mix lightly to avoid compacting and ensure tender meatballs. Shape into 1-inch balls. Sauté the meatballs in the olive oil in a skillet until cooked through and brown.

For the soup, sauté the onion in the butter in a 3-quart saucepan over medium heat for 3 minutes or until tender. Add the beef broth, water, undrained tomatoes, oregano and sugar; use the back of a wooden spoon to break up the tomatoes.

Bring to a boil over medium heat and reduce the heat to low. Simmer for 8 to 10 minutes or until the flavours blend. Add the green beans and simmer for 3 minutes. Stir in the pasta and add the meatballs. Simmer for 15 minutes or until the pasta is tender, stirring occasionally. Ladle into soup bowls and sprinkle with Parmesan cheese if desired.

You may prepare the soup in advance, adding the pasta and green beans when it is reheated to serve.

Serves 8   *Pamela Shaw*

Bermuda Fish Chowder

1 (2-pound) whole rockfish, yellowtail or hogfish, or 1 (24-ounce) fillet
1 bay leaf
9 cups water
1/2 pound potatoes, peeled and chopped
1/2 pound onions, chopped
1 (14-ounce) can chopped tomatoes
1 cup chopped carrots
1/2 cup chopped celery
1/2 ounce chopped parsley
1 tablespoon Worcestershire sauce
1 tablespoon soy sauce
3 cubes fish bouillon
1 tablespoon chopped thyme
1 teaspoon salt
5 tablespoons rum
11/2 teaspoons sherry pepper sauce

Cook the fish with the bay leaf in the water in a saucepan for 1 hour; drain, returning the fish stock to the saucepan. Add the potatoes and onions to the fish stock and cook until they start to become tender. Add the tomatoes, carrots, celery, parsley, Worcestershire sauce, soy sauce, fish bouillon, thyme and salt.

Break the fish fillet into pieces and measure 3 cups. Add to the saucepan. Simmer over low heat for 2 hours, stirring occasionally. Stir in the rum and sherry pepper sauce. Ladle into soup bowls, discarding the bay leaf.

You may sauté the carrots and celery before adding them to the soup if desired. Bermudians traditionally cook the fish whole with the head, tail and bones, fillet the fish and for flavour add the head and bones back to the soup while simmering. Remove head and bones prior to serving.

Serves 6

Cornelia Kempe

Mixed Seafood Chowder

5 slices bacon, cut into $1/2$-inch pieces
1 large onion, chopped
1 garlic clove, minced
$1/3$ cup chopped parsley
1 cup clam juice
1 cup fish stock or chicken stock
2 large potatoes, peeled and cut into $1/2$-inch pieces
8 ounces scallops

1 pound fish fillets, such as halibut, sole or rockfish
2 cups milk
2 cups half-and-half
10 ounces baby clams
8 ounces small shrimp, cooked
salt and pepper to taste
coriander leaves

Fry the bacon until crisp in a 5- to 6-quart saucepan. Remove the bacon with a slotted spoon and pour off all but 2 tablespoons of the bacon drippings. Add the onion, garlic and parsley to the drippings in the saucepan and sauté for 10 minutes or until the onion is tender. Add the clam juice, fish stock and potatoes.

Bring to a boil and reduce the heat. Cook, covered, for 10 to 15 minutes or until the potatoes are almost tender. Add the scallops and fish fillets. Simmer, covered, for 5 minutes or until the thickest part of the fish flakes easily with a fork.

Stir in the milk, half-and-half, undrained clams, shrimp and bacon. Heat to serving temperature over low heat, stirring occasionally; do not boil. Season with salt and pepper. Ladle into soup bowls and garnish with coriander leaves.

Serves 8

Sally Gibbons

Paw Paw Salad

WHITE WINE VINAIGRETTE

2 tablespoons white wine vinegar
$1/4$ cup sunflower oil
1 tablespoon mayonnaise
1 garlic clove, crushed
1 teaspoon salt
$1/2$ teaspoon pepper

SALAD

4 cups grated green paw paw
2 tablespoons chopped parsley
2 tablespoons freshly squeezed lime juice

For the vinaigrette, combine the vinegar, sunflower oil and mayonnaise in a bowl and whisk until smooth. Whisk in the garlic, salt and pepper. Chill until serving time.

For the salad, toss the paw paw with the vinaigrette in a serving bowl. Sprinkle with the parsley and drizzle with the lime juice.

Bermudians refer to the papaya as paw paw.

Serves 6

Deborah Titterton Narraway

FIRST PROJECT   *In 1937, BJSL's first major project was the establishment of the Victoria Lodge home for underprivileged children. Their operation of this project was continued until 1945.*

Island Fruit Salad

FRUIT SALAD DRESSING

1 cup water
1 mango tea bag
1 tablespoon sugar
juice of 1/2 lime

SALAD

1 mango, chopped
1 orange, chopped
1/4 cantaloupe, chopped
1/4 honeydew, chopped
1/4 pineapple, chopped
1 large watermelon wedge, chopped
1 large banana
thin slivers of lime peel

For the dressing, bring the water to a boil in a small saucepan. Add the tea bag and let stand for 5 minutes. Remove the tea bag and stir in the sugar and lime juice. Chill until serving time.

For the salad, combine the mango, orange, cantaloupe, honeydew, pineapple and watermelon in a bowl and mix well; chill until serving time. Slice the banana at serving time and add to the salad; mix gently. Spoon into serving bowls and drizzle with the dressing. Top with slivers of lime peel.

This makes a beautiful presentation in pineapple boats or even a carved watermelon half. You can then use the fruit in the salad.

Serves 4

Louise Gibbons

Greek Village Salad

GREEK DRESSING

1/2 cup olive oil
1/4 cup vinegar
1 large garlic clove, minced
2 tablespoons chopped fresh parsley
pinch of dried oregano

SALAD

4 medium tomatoes, cut into wedges
1 medium cucumber, sliced diagonally
1 small green bell pepper, thinly sliced
5 green onions, sliced
5 radishes, sliced
15 green olives or black olives
1/2 head romaine lettuce, torn
2 teaspoons dried dill weed, or 2 tablespoons chopped fresh dill weed
salt and pepper to taste
1 cup (4 ounces) crumbled feta cheese

For the dressing, combine the olive oil, vinegar, garlic, parsley and oregano in a small jar and shake to mix well. Store in the refrigerator until serving time.

For the salad, combine the tomatoes, cucumber, bell pepper, green onions, radishes and olives in a large shallow salad bowl. Add the lettuce, dill weed, salt and pepper and toss to mix well. Add the dressing and toss gently to coat well. Sprinkle with the feta cheese.

You should always wash, dry and chill lettuce ahead of time for crunchy salads. Remember to always tear lettuce gently rather than cutting it.

Serves 8

Kathy Suter

Coleslaw

1 (16-ounce) can pineapple tidbits
1 small cabbage, finely shredded
1 bunch fresh parsley, chopped
3 tablespoons mayonnaise
1 teaspoon sugar
1 teaspoon salt

Drain the pineapple, reserving the juice. Combine the pineapple with the cabbage and parsley in a bowl and mix well. Blend the mayonnaise, sugar and salt with the desired amount of the reserved pineapple juice. Add to the cabbage mixture and mix well. Chill until the flavours blend.

Serves 6

Tammy Gibbons

Junkyard Salad

1 green bell pepper
1 red bell pepper
1 yellow bell pepper
1 orange bell pepper
4 plum tomatoes
olive oil
salt and pepper to taste
1 small onion, sliced
1 tablespoon butter
1 head red leaf butter lettuce, torn
1/2 cup (2 ounces) crumbled feta cheese
1/2 cup slivered almonds, lightly toasted
Vidalia onion or raspberry walnut vinaigrette

Roast and skin the bell peppers using the instructions in the sidebar on this page. Cut the tomatoes into halves and sprinkle with olive oil, salt and pepper. Place on a baking sheet on the lowest oven shelf and roast while the peppers are roasting. Reduce the oven temperature to 250 degrees when the peppers are removed from the oven and roast for 1 1/2 hours longer or until the tomatoes are dried. Slice the roasted peppers into thin strips and cut the tomato halves into quarters.

Sauté the onion in the butter in a skillet over low heat until caramelised. Combine the onion with the lettuce, tomatoes and peppers in a bowl and mix well. Top with the feta cheese and toasted almonds. Drizzle with vinaigrette and toss to coat well.

You may add prosciutto or other roasted or grilled vegetables, such as zucchini, summer squash and eggplant, to this salad or substitute goat cheese for the feta cheese and toasted pine nuts for the almonds. Have fun and use your imagination and whatever you have on hand.

Serves 6

Dawn Dunstan

ROASTED PEPPERS

Roasted peppers are delicious in salads or sandwiches or served as a side dish topped with goat cheese. To roast peppers, remove the stems and seeds from bell peppers and place on a broiler pan or grill. Broil or grill for 15 to 20 minutes or until evenly charred on all sides; the skins should bubble and blacken, but the flesh should not burn. Place in a sealable plastic bag and seal; let stand until cool and slip off the skins. Slice or prepare as needed for the recipe.

Cup Match Potato Salad

3 pounds red potatoes
6 hard-cooked eggs, chopped
1 red onion, chopped
1 cup frozen green peas, thawed
1 small bunch parsley, chopped
2 tablespoons mayonnaise

$^1/_2$ teaspoon paprika
1 teaspoon sugar
salt to taste
2 teaspoons garlic pepper
parsley sprigs, fresh thyme and/or cherry tomatoes
1 hard-cooked egg, sliced

Combine the unpeeled potatoes with enough water to cover in a saucepan. Cook until the potatoes are fork tender. Drain and cool the potatoes; cut into chunks. Combine with the eggs, onion, peas and parsley in a bowl and mix well.

Blend the mayonnaise, paprika, sugar, salt and garlic pepper in a bowl and mix well. Add to the potato mixture and mix gently. Garnish with additional parsley sprigs, fresh thyme and/or cherry tomatoes. You may also sprinkle with additional paprika and top with slices of additional hard-cooked egg.

Serves 6 to 8

Tammy Gibbons

Pesto Potato Salad

1 pound small new potatoes
1/2 cup mayonnaise
1/3 cup sour cream
1/2 cup pine nuts
1 cup chopped fresh basil
2 garlic cloves, minced
1 cup (4 ounces) grated Parmesan cheese

Combine the potatoes with enough water to cover in a saucepan and cook just until tender. Drain and let stand, covered with a kitchen towel, until cool.

Combine the mayonnaise, sour cream, pine nuts, basil, garlic and Parmesan cheese in a food processor and process until smooth. Adjust the amounts to suit taste and thicken, if necessary, with additional cheese.

Combine the dressing and potatoes in a bowl and mix gently. Garnish with additional pine nuts, Parmesan cheese and basil. Chill until serving time.

Serves 6

Beth Lindgren

WASHING FRESH SPINACH

To prepare fresh spinach for a salad, first trim the stems. Fill the sink with cold water and submerge each bunch in the water, swishing vigorously. Remove the spinach, replace the water and repeat the process until the water is clear. Dry the spinach well before using in the salad so the dressing will adhere.

BALSAMIC VINAIGRETTE

1/4 cup olive oil
1 tablespoon balsamic vinegar
2 teaspoons whole grain mustard, or to taste
1 to 2 teaspoons honey, or to taste

SALAD

1 package fresh baby spinach
12 cherry tomatoes, cut into halves
4 large portobello mushrooms, thickly sliced
chopped garlic to taste
butter
1/4 cup sweetened dried cranberries
1/4 cup pine nuts

For the vinaigrette, combine the olive oil, balsamic vinegar, mustard and honey in a bowl and whisk until smooth. Store in the refrigerator.

For the salad, combine the spinach and cherry tomatoes in a salad bowl and toss to mix well. Sauté the mushrooms and garlic in a small amount of butter in a skillet. Spread the warm mushrooms over the salad and sprinkle with the cranberries and pine nuts. Drizzle with the vinaigrette and serve immediately.

Serves 4 to 6   *Lesley Page*

Spinach Salad

with Peanuts and Apple

CHUTNEY DRESSING

1/4 cup fresh lemon juice
2 tablespoons red wine vinegar
5 tablespoons mango chutney
1/2 teaspoon sugar
1 teaspoon curry powder
1/2 teaspoon turmeric
salt and black pepper to taste
1/2 teaspoon cayenne pepper or paprika
1 cup canola oil

SALAD

1 bunch spinach
2 green or yellow apples, coarsely chopped
1 bunch scallions, chopped
1 1/2 cups roasted whole peanuts

For the dressing, combine the lemon juice, red wine vinegar, chutney, sugar, curry powder, turmeric, salt, black pepper and cayenne pepper in a blender and process for 2 minutes. Add the canola oil gradually, processing constantly until smooth. Store in the refrigerator.

For the salad, combine the spinach with the apples, scallions and peanuts in a salad bowl and toss to mix. Add the dressing at serving time and toss to coat evenly.

If you combine the salad ingredients in advance, toss the apples with lemon juice to prevent browning.

Serves 6   *Susan Ternent*

Pear Salad

with Prosciutto and Stilton

DIJON DRESSING

2 tablespoons white wine vinegar
1/2 teaspoon Dijon mustard
salt and pepper to taste
1/4 cup olive oil

SALAD

1/2 cup chopped pecans
6 cups red or green leaf Boston lettuce
2 large red Bartlett pears with skins, cut into wedges
6 thin slices prosciutto, cut into strips
1 cup (4 ounces) crumbled Stilton cheese

For the dressing, whisk the white wine vinegar, Dijon mustard, salt and pepper in a bowl until smooth. Whisk in the olive oil gradually. Store in the refrigerator.

For the salad, sprinkle the pecans in a skillet. Toast over medium heat just until golden brown, stirring frequently. Cool to room temperature.

Toss the lettuce with half the dressing in a salad bowl. Arrange on 6 serving plates. Arrange the pear wedges and prosciutto over the lettuce. Drizzle with the remaining dressing and sprinkle with the Stilton cheese and pecans.

Serves 6

Dawn Dunstan

Chicken and Avocado Salad

BALSAMIC VINAIGRETTE

6 tablespoons olive oil
2 tablespoons balsamic vinegar
2 tablespoons white wine vinegar
3 tablespoons mayonnaise
2 teaspoons English mustard
2 teaspoons honey
1/4 teaspoon salt
1/2 teaspoon pepper

SALAD

8 ounces arugula or baby spinach
3 ripe avocados, sliced
3 chicken breasts, roasted, cooled
  and sliced
4 ounces pine nuts or chopped peanuts
18 cherry tomatoes

For the vinaigrette, combine the olive oil, balsamic vinegar, white wine vinegar, mayonnaise, mustard and honey in a bowl and whisk until smooth. Whisk in the salt and pepper. Store in the refrigerator.

For the salad, arrange the arugula leaves on a serving platter. Arrange the avocado slices over the arugula. Top with the chicken slices. Drizzle with the vinaigrette and sprinkle with the pine nuts. Arrange the cherry tomatoes over the top and serve immediately.

Serves 6

Louise Gibbons

Flank Steak Salad

1 cup teriyaki sauce
3 garlic cloves, crushed
1 (1-inch) piece gingerroot, peeled and chopped
1 flank steak
salt and pepper to taste
Roasted Summer Vegetables (page 183), chilled

Mix the teriyaki sauce, garlic and gingerroot in a shallow dish or large sealable plastic bag. Add the steak and cover or seal. Marinate in the refrigerator for 8 hours or longer.

Drain the steak, reserving the marinade. Sprinkle the steak with salt and pepper. Grill over medium coals for 4 minutes on each side for medium, brushing with the reserved marinade. Chill until serving time.

Cut the steak diagonally across the grain into very thin slices. Serve with Roasted Summer Vegetables.

You may also cook the steak in a small amount of oil in a large heavy saucepan over medium-high heat until done to taste if preferred.

Serves 8

Joe Gibbons

BERMUDA RED CROSS *In 1952, BJSL assisted the Bermuda Red Cross with a project to collect blood type data on 6,000 people in Bermuda.*

Shrimp and Pasta Salad

SESAME SOY DRESSING

1 cup mayonnaise
$^1/_3$ cup soy sauce
2 tablespoons sesame oil or olive oil
$1^1/_2$ teaspoons Dijon mustard
1 garlic clove, minced
1 tablespoon crushed dried chile

SALAD

16 ounces uncooked pasta
8 ounces shrimp, cooked and peeled
$^1/_4$ cup snow peas or fresh green beans
1 red or yellow bell pepper, thinly sliced
1 carrot, chopped
3 green onions, chopped
$^1/_2$ cup sliced water chestnuts
$^1/_4$ cup chopped fresh coriander leaves

For the dressing, combine the mayonnaise, soy sauce, sesame oil, Dijon mustard, garlic and chile in a bowl and mix well. Store in the refrigerator.

For the salad, cook the pasta al dente using the package directions; drain and cool. Combine with the shrimp, snow peas, bell pepper, carrot, green onions and water chestnuts in a large salad bowl and mix well. Add the dressing and toss to coat evenly. Sprinkle with the coriander.

You can minimize the odor of cooking shrimp by adding celery leaves to the water.

Serves 4 to 6

Tegan Smith

Asian Pasta Salad

ASIAN DRESSING

2 tablespoons cider vinegar
2 tablespoons light soy sauce
1 tablespoon extra-virgin olive oil
2 garlic cloves, crushed
1$^{1}/_{2}$ teaspoons chopped gingerroot
1 teaspoon sugar or an equivalent amount of
　artificial sweetener

SALAD

1 cup frozen green peas, thawed
$^{1}/_{2}$ medium red bell pepper, chopped
$^{1}/_{2}$ medium yellow bell pepper, chopped
$^{1}/_{2}$ medium orange bell pepper, chopped
$^{1}/_{2}$ cup shredded carrot
$^{1}/_{2}$ cup sliced celery
4 cups cooked bow tie pasta, cooled

For the dressing, whisk the cider vinegar, soy sauce and olive oil in a bowl until smooth. Add the garlic, gingerroot and sugar and mix well.

For the salad, combine the peas, bell peppers, carrot and celery in a bowl and mix well. Add the pasta and dressing and toss to mix well. Chill for 2 hours before serving.

Serves 6

Kendra Wharton

Rice Salad

CURRY DRESSING

1/2 cup vegetable oil
3 tablespoons soy sauce
2 tablespoons white vinegar
1 tablespoon curry powder

SALAD

1 (7-ounce) package long grain and wild rice mix
2 small onions, chopped
1 green bell pepper, chopped
3 ribs celery, sliced
2 cups frozen green peas, thawed
1 bunch broccoli, chopped
1 pint mushrooms, sliced
1 cup dry Chinese noodles

For the dressing, combine the oil, soy sauce, white vinegar and curry powder in a jar and shake until well mixed. Store in the refrigerator.

For the salad, cook the rice using the package directions. Cool to room temperature. Combine the rice with the onions, bell pepper, celery, peas, broccoli and mushrooms in a bowl and mix gently. Add the dressing and toss to mix well.

Chill for 24 hours, stirring occasionally. Sprinkle with the Chinese noodles at serving time if desired.

Serves 6

Elizabeth Parker

Entrées

Salmon Wellington

**FROZEN
PUFF PASTRY**

*Frozen puff pastry is
readily available in most
grocery stores and is a
wonderful time-saver.
Consult the package
directions to determine
whether the frozen puff
pastry is pre-rolled or not.
If not, additional rolling on
a lightly floured surface
will be necessary. Use a
rolling pin and strive for
a consistent thickness of
about one-eighth inch. If
the recipe calls for smaller
pieces of pastry, use a long
sharp knife to cut it.*

1 (2-pound) salmon fillet
1/2 cup chopped onion
1/2 cup chopped celery
butter
2 cups fresh bread crumbs or
  stuffing

thyme or tarragon to taste
2 sheets frozen puff pastry, thawed
1 egg yolk
1 tablespoon water

Wrap the salmon in foil and
place on a baking sheet.
Bake at 400 degrees for
20 minutes or until the fish
flakes easily. Let stand until
cool. Reduce the oven
temperature to 350 degrees.

Sauté the onion and celery
in a small amount of butter
in a skillet. Combine with
the bread crumbs in a bowl
and season with thyme and
tarragon. Add just enough
water to moisten the mixture.

Roll 1 sheet of the puff pastry
on a lightly floured work
surface. Place the salmon

on the pastry. Mound the stuffing mixture on the salmon. Roll the remaining sheet
of puff pastry on a work surface and place over the salmon. Brush the edges
with a mixture of the egg yolk and 1 tablespoon water; press the edges to seal.
Slash the top in a decorative pattern and brush with the remaining egg wash.

Place on a baking sheet and bake at 350 degrees for 30 minutes or until
golden brown; cover loosely with foil if necessary to prevent overbrowning.
Serve with wild rice and fiddleheads sautéed in butter and sprinkled with
Parmesan cheese.

You may also stuff the salmon with wild rice or sauté shrimp with the onion
and celery and add to the bread crumb stuffing.

Serves 6 to 8

Cornelia Kempe

Grilled Salmon Fillets

1 cup sake or rice wine vinegar
^{1}/2 cup soy sauce
1 tablespoon dark brown sugar
2 garlic cloves, crushed
1 tablespoon crushed gingerroot
6 salmon fillets
Fresh Tomato Salsa (below)

Combine the sake, soy sauce, brown sugar, garlic and gingerroot in a bowl and mix well. Add the salmon fillets and marinate in the refrigerator for 2 hours or longer; drain.

Grill over high heat for 7 to 8 minutes or just until the fish flakes easily; do not overcook. Serve with the Fresh Tomato Salsa.

You may also place the salmon in a broiler pan and broil for 10 minutes or until the fish flakes easily.

Serves 6   *Carolyn Toogood*

Fresh Tomato Salsa

1 pint (2 cups) cherry tomatoes, cut into quarters
8 garlic cloves, chopped
^{1}/2 cup pine nuts, chopped
^{1}/2 cup fresh basil leaves, chopped
1 tablespoon virgin olive oil
salt and freshly ground pepper to taste

Combine the cherry tomatoes, garlic, pine nuts and basil in a large bowl and mix well. Stir in the olive oil and season with salt and pepper. Store in a covered container in the refrigerator for up to 3 days. Serve with fresh fish or grilled steak or as an appetizer with fresh bread and cheese or tortilla chips.

Makes 2^1/2 cups   *Rosalind Gutteridge*

Tuna Steaks

TUNA STEAKS

1/2 cup vegetable oil
chopped fresh dill weed to taste
pepper to taste
6 tuna steaks

WASABI SAUCE

6 tablespoons (3/4 stick) butter
3 green onions, finely chopped
1 teaspoon chopped parsley
1 tablespoon (or more) wasabi paste
3 tablespoons soy sauce
1 1/2 tablespoons fresh lime juice
pepper to taste

For the tuna, mix the oil, dill weed and pepper in a small bowl. Coat the tuna with the mixture and place in a shallow dish. Marinate in the refrigerator for 20 minutes. Grill until the fish flakes easily.

For the sauce, melt the butter in a saucepan and add the green onions, parsley, wasabi paste, soy sauce, lime juice and pepper. Cook over low heat until the sauce is thickened and smooth, whisking constantly; do not boil. Serve with the tuna.

Serves 6

Sue Sharpe

KIDS ON THE BLOCK *In 1990, BJSL started a programme using puppets to teach school children about disabilities. BJSL ran this programme for nine years before turning it over to WindReach Recreational Village.*

Curried Mussel Pie

FILLING

1 large onion, minced
3 carrots, chopped
2 potatoes, peeled and chopped
3 garlic cloves, minced
3 tablespoons curry powder
pinch of thyme
vegetable oil
1 fish bouillon cube
1 tablespoon sugar
salt and pepper to taste
2 cups roux
3 pounds fresh Bermuda mussels from
    Baileys Bay
1 cup frozen peas

CURRY PASTRY

4 cups flour
2 teaspoons sugar
1 teaspoon curry powder
$1/4$ teaspoon salt
2 cups (4 sticks) butter, softened
1 egg, beaten

For the filling, sauté the onion, carrots, potatoes, garlic, curry powder and thyme in a small amount of oil in a saucepan. Add the fish bouillon cube and enough water to cover the vegetables. Stir in the sugar and season with salt and pepper. Cook until the vegetables are tender. Stir in the roux and cook until the mixture thickens, stirring constantly. Stir in the mussels and peas.

For the pastry, sift the flour, sugar, curry powder and salt into a bowl. Add the butter and mix with a pastry blender until crumbly. Make a well in the center and add water 1 drop at a time until the mixture forms a dough. Divide into 8 portions.

Roll 4 portions on a lightly floured surface and fit into 4 greased small pie plates. Spoon the filling into the prepared plates. Roll the remaining dough on a lightly floured surface and fit over the filling. Seal and crimp the edges and cut a circle in the center to vent. Brush with the beaten egg. Bake at 350 degrees for 1 hour or until golden brown.

You may also prepare this in a 9×13-inch baking dish.

Serves 8

Tammy Gibbons

Removing the dark vein that runs along the back of the shrimp is done simply for aesthetic reasons. Peeled uncooked shrimp are deveined by running a small knife along the back of the shrimp, taking care not to cut too deeply. Lift the vein up gently with the tip of the knife and remove it. There may be times when you want to devein shrimp in the shell. This is most easily done by slitting the shell with a knife and removing the vein in the same manner.

Shrimp Curry

1 English cucumber
2 pounds uncooked shrimp, peeled
$^1/_4$ cup ($^1/_2$ stick) butter
1 (4-ounce) can pimentos, drained and cut into strips
$^1/_4$ cup ketchup
1 to 2 teaspoons curry powder
1 cup milk
$1^1/_2$ tablespoons cornstarch
2 tablespoons sherry

Peel the cucumber and cut lengthwise into 8 strips; cut the strips into quarters. Sauté the shrimp in the butter in a saucepan for 3 minutes. Add the cucumber and pimentos and cook, covered, for 3 minutes. Stir in the ketchup, curry powder and $^2/_3$ cup of the milk.

Blend the remaining $^1/_3$ cup milk with the cornstarch in a cup. Add to the shrimp mixture and bring to a boil, stirring constantly. Reduce the heat. Cook until thickened, stirring constantly. Stir in the sherry. Serve over rice.

Serves 4   *Betty Kempe*

Bouillabaisse

8 ounces canned tomatoes or chopped fresh tomatoes
2 tablespoons tomato paste
1¹/₂ cups fish stock
1 cup white wine
1 Bermuda onion or 6 scallions, chopped
2 or 3 garlic cloves, crushed
1 pound tilapia or other white fish, cut into 1-inch pieces
8 sea scallops, cut into halves
12 green olives
2 teaspoons hot sauce
1 tablespoon chopped fresh dill weed
1 teaspoon dried oregano
1 teaspoon dried thyme
16 mussels
16 large shrimp, peeled and deveined

Cook the tomatoes in a large saucepan over low heat until they begin to break apart. Stir in the tomato paste, fish stock, wine, onion and garlic. Increase the heat and bring to a boil. Reduce the heat to medium and cook for 5 minutes.

Add the fish, scallops, olives, hot sauce, dill weed, oregano and thyme. Simmer for 15 minutes. Add the mussels and cook until the shells open. Add the shrimp and simmer for 10 minutes longer. Ladle into soup bowls and serve with warmed and buttered crusty French bread.

You may prepare this dish with thawed frozen fish and shellfish. It is a good way to prepare a quick, impressive dinner with ingredients from the pantry and freezer.

Serves 4   *Louise Gibbons*

WOMEN'S HOSPITAL AUXILIARY   *In 1953, BJSL was approached to assist in the formation of a hospital auxiliary. Today, the Women's Hospital Auxiliary is an indispensable organisation.*

Seafood Medley

1 cup uncooked fusilli
1 small onion, chopped
1 rib celery, chopped
2 garlic cloves, crushed
1 tablespoon olive oil
8 ounces uncooked shrimp, peeled
8 ounces haddock or other white fish, cut into
 1-inch pieces

2 tablespoons mixed chopped fresh basil,
 oregano and thyme
1/2 cup dry white wine
1 (14-ounce) can chopped tomatoes
3 ounces fresh spinach
grated Parmesan cheese

Cook the pasta using the package directions; drain. Sauté the onion, celery and garlic in the olive oil in a saucepan for 5 minutes or until the vegetables are tender. Add the shrimp, fish and mixed herbs. Cook until the shrimp turn pink.

Add the wine and tomatoes and simmer for 15 minutes, stirring occasionally. Add the spinach and pasta and mix well. Cook just until the spinach wilts. Spoon into a serving bowl and top with Parmesan cheese.

You may also use the fresh spinach to line the serving plate if preferred.

Serves 4

Melanie Dupres

Rare Roast Beef

with Fluffy Horseradish Sauce

1/4 cup horseradish, drained
1 cup sour cream
1 tablespoon lemon juice
1 tablespoon sugar

1 tablespoon minced chives
1 (6- to 8-pound) standing rib roast
salt and pepper to taste
Yorkshire Pudding (below)

Mix the horseradish, sour cream, lemon juice, sugar and chives in a bowl for the horseradish sauce. Chill, covered, for several hours.

Rub the roast on all sides with salt and pepper. Place rib side down on a rack in a roasting pan. Roast at 375 degrees for 1 hour. Turn off the oven, but do not open the oven door. Let the roast stand in the oven for 3 to 5 hours.

Set the oven temperature to 375 degrees and roast again for 30 minutes for rare or for 45 minutes for medium. Let stand for 15 minutes before carving. Serve with the horseradish sauce and Yorkshire Pudding.

This method of cooking can be used for a roast of up to 10 pounds.

Serves 8

Wendi Ryland

Yorkshire Pudding

2 cups flour
2 eggs
2 cups milk

salt to taste
vegetable oil

Combine the flour, eggs, milk and salt in a blender and process until smooth. Let stand for 2 hours. Spread a small amount of oil in a 9×13-inch baking dish. Place in a 425-degree oven and heat until hot. Add the batter and bake for 25 to 30 minutes. Serve with roast beef. You can reheat leftovers and serve with warm treacle as a dessert.

Serves 9

Susan Titterton

YORKSHIRE PUDDING

The English classic, roast beef with Yorkshire pudding, is also traditional in Bermuda. Yorkshire pudding, made from the same batter used to make popovers, is baked in the oven along with the meat it will accompany. If the meat is roasted on a spit, the Yorkshire pudding is placed below the meat so that the drippings flavour the top of the pudding. Alternatively, Yorkshire pudding can be made by incorporating some of the meat drippings into the pudding batter. By either method, this savoury pudding provides a lovely complement to roast beef.

Exotic Beef Curry

1 onion, chopped
2 garlic cloves, chopped
1 fresh red chile, chopped
1 (1-inch) piece gingerroot
1 pound sirloin steak
1 tablespoon olive oil
1 teaspoon ground coriander

1 teaspoon ground cumin
5 medium tomatoes, peeled and cut into quarters
1 (10-ounce) can beef stock
1/2 (14-ounce) can light coconut milk
1 tablespoon soy sauce
1 teaspoon sugar
1 tablespoon unsalted peanuts

Combine the onion, garlic, chile and gingerroot in a food processor and process to a paste. Cut the steak into 1-inch cubes. Sauté the beef in the olive oil in a saucepan until brown on all sides but not cooked through. Remove the steak with a slotted spoon.

Add the paste to the skillet and sauté lightly. Stir in the coriander and cumin and sauté for 3 minutes over low heat. Add the steak, tomatoes, beef stock, coconut milk, soy sauce and sugar and mix well.

Simmer over low heat for 30 to 40 minutes or until the beef is tender. Spoon into a serving bowl and sprinkle with the peanuts. Garnish with additional coriander. Serve with jasmine rice.

You may prepare the dish in advance and reheat to serve. The unused portion of coconut milk can be frozen in ice cube trays and stored in plastic bags in the freezer for the next beef curry dish.

Serves 4

Louise Gibbons

Beef Fajitas

FAJITA MARINADE

1/2 cup balsamic vinegar or red wine vinegar
1/4 cup freshly squeezed lime juice
2 tablespoons dark soy sauce
4 or 5 large garlic cloves, crushed
1/4 cup coarsely chopped coriander leaves
1 tablespoon chili powder
2 teaspoons salt
1/2 teaspoon red pepper flakes

FAJITAS

2 pounds skirt steak
1 large onion, sliced into strips
2 small green bell peppers, sliced into strips
chopped or crushed garlic cloves
olive oil
1 package small or large tortillas
1 cup (4 ounces) shredded Cheddar cheese
1 small container sour cream
salsa or guacamole

For the marinade, combine the balsamic vinegar, lime juice, soy sauce, garlic, coriander leaves, chili powder, salt and pepper flakes in a shallow dish.

For the fajitas, pound the steak on both sides with a meat mallet to tenderize it. Add to the marinade and let stand in the refrigerator for 4 hours or longer; drain. Grill the steak until done to taste. Slice at a 45-degree angle into thin strips.

Sauté the onion, bell peppers and garlic in a small amount of olive oil in a skillet. Combine with the beef strips in a bowl and serve with the tortillas, Cheddar cheese, sour cream and salsa or guacamole.

Serves 6

Wendi Ryland

Grilled Marinated Steak

1/2 cup virgin olive oil
2 tablespoons balsamic vinegar
2 tablespoons soy sauce
2 teaspoons lemon juice
2 tablespoons Worcestershire sauce
2 teaspoons Dijon mustard
1 teaspoon basil
1 teaspoon thyme
1 teaspoon garlic powder, or to taste
1 tablespoon salt
1 tablespoon pepper
4 (1-inch) T-bone steaks

Combine the olive oil, balsamic vinegar, soy sauce, lemon juice, Worcestershire sauce, Dijon mustard, basil, thyme, garlic powder, salt and pepper in a bowl and mix well for the marinade.

Place each steak in a sealable plastic bag. Divide the marinade evenly between the bags and seal; knead to coat the steaks well. Marinate the steaks in the refrigerator for up to 24 hours.

Drain the steaks, reserving the marinade. Grill or broil the steaks until done to taste, basting with the reserved marinade.

You may also use this marinade for a roast.

Serves 4

Kim Paterson

Marinated Grilled Lamb

1 cup red wine
1 cup beef stock
3 tablespoons orange marlamade
2 tablespoons wine vinegar
1 tablespoon minced onion
2 garlic cloves, minced
1 tablespoon dried or fresh rosemary
1 tablespoon marjoram
2 bay leaves
1/4 teaspoon ground ginger
salt and pepper to taste
1 (5- to 6-pound) leg of lamb, boned and butterflied
Grilled Peaches (at right)

Combine the wine, beef stock, marmalade and wine vinegar in a saucepan
for the marinade. Stir in the onion, garlic, rosemary, marjoram, bay leaves,
ginger, salt and pepper. Simmer for 20 minutes, stirring occasionally. Cool for
10 minutes.

Place the lamb in a deep dish and pour the marinade over the lamb. Cover
with plastic wrap and marinate in the refrigerator for 4 hours or longer.

Drain the lamb, reserving the marinade. Place fat side up on a grill over
medium coals. Grill for 1 hour, basting frequently with the reserved marinade
and turning the lamb to grill evenly. Serve with Grilled Peaches, a spinach
salad and saffron rice.

Serves 6   *Susan Ternent*

GRILLED PEACHES

Peaches are delicious cooked on the grill. Simply wash the peaches and cut them into halves. Discard the stones and brush the cut surfaces with butter. Grill them until the skins are lightly charred and the flesh is soft. Leftovers are delicious served cold. Grilled peaches are also good in a tossed salad.

Pork Tenderloin

with Pineapple Marinade

¹/₄ fresh pineapple
2 tablespoons olive oil
juice of 1 lemon
4 garlic cloves

1 teaspoon pepper
1 pork tenderloin
2 tablespoons soy sauce
¹/₃ cup Cointreau or sherry

Combine the pineapple, olive oil, lemon juice, garlic and pepper in a blender. Process to form a smooth paste. Tie the pork with kitchen twine and rub with the pineapple mixture. Place in a covered container and marinate in the refrigerator for 8 hours or longer.

Grill the tenderloin until done to taste, drizzling with the soy sauce during the last 5 minutes and with the Cointreau during the last minute of grilling time.

You may also grill strips of fresh pineapple to serve with the tenderloin.

Serves 6

Julia Bolton

Marinated Pork Tenderloin

1/4 cup soy sauce
3 tablespoons vegetable oil
1 garlic clove, minced
1/2 cup sliced green onions
3 tablespoons sesame seeds
2 teaspoons brown sugar
1/4 teaspoon ground ginger
1/4 teaspoon pepper
1 pork tenderloin

Mix the soy sauce, oil, garlic, green onions, sesame seeds, brown sugar, ginger and pepper in a shallow dish. Tie the tenderloin with kitchen twine. Add to the marinade and turn to coat evenly. Marinate in the refrigerator for 24 hours.

Drain the tenderloin, discarding the marinade. Grill, covered, for 12 to 15 minutes or until cooked through, turning once.

Serves 6   Kelly Marshall

TOO HOT TO COOK?

Prepare fresh vegetables and even fruits alongside the meat you are grilling. Wrap green beans, asparagus or other vegetables in heavy-duty foil and add a small amount of water and butter or oil and seasonings. Place them on the edges of the grill and allow to steam for 5 to 10 minutes or until done to taste, turning frequently.

Pork with Caramelised Apples

2 apples
2 tablespoons butter
1 tablespoon brown sugar
1 teaspoon olive oil
4 pork loin steaks
1/4 cup crème fraîche
1 tablespoon chopped sage or thyme
salt and pepper to taste

Cut each apple into 8 wedges, discarding the cores. Melt the butter with the brown sugar in a skillet and mix well. Add the apples to the skillet and cook over low heat for 5 to 10 minutes or until caramelised. Remove with a slotted spoon and keep warm.

Add the olive oil to the skillet and heat over medium heat. Add the steaks and cook for 5 minutes on each side. Stir in the crème fraîche, sage, salt and pepper. Cook just until heated through. Serve over steamed vegetables. Top with the apples and spoon the cooking juices over the top.

Serves 4   *Kim Moseley*

Pork Chops in Apricot Sauce

6 boneless pork chops
1 (8-ounce) can apricots in syrup
4 ounces fresh mushrooms, sliced
2 tablespoons sliced green onions

1 (10-ounce) can cream of
  chicken soup
1/2 cup sour cream
1/2 cup sliced almonds, toasted

Spray a large skillet with nonstick cooking spray and heat over high heat.
Add the pork chops and cook until light brown on both sides. Drain the
apricots, reserving 1/3 cup of the syrup. Add the reserved syrup, mushrooms,
green onions, soup and sour cream to the skillet. Reduce the heat and cook,
covered, for 25 minutes, stirring occasionally. Stir in the apricots and almonds
and cook for 5 minutes longer. Serve over rice.

Serves 6

Elysa Burland

Pork Chops in Mustard Sauce

4 pork chops
1 large onion, thinly sliced
2 garlic cloves, minced
1 cup apple cider or apple juice
3 tablespoons Dijon mustard

1/2 teaspoon dried thyme, or
  1 1/2 teaspoons chopped
  fresh thyme
1/2 teaspoon salt
1/4 teaspoon pepper

Brown the pork chops on both sides in a medium nonstick skillet; remove to a
plate. Add the onion and garlic and sauté until tender. Return the pork chops
to the skillet and spoon the onion mixture over the top. Mix the apple cider,
Dijon mustard, thyme, salt and pepper in a small bowl. Pour over the pork
chops. Bring to a boil over high heat. Reduce the heat and simmer, covered,
for 15 minutes. Remove the pork chops and onion mixture to a serving plate.
Increase the heat to high and cook until the sauce is reduced to the desired
thickness. Pour over the pork chops.

Serves 4

Diane Steiger

TOASTING NUTS

Sprinkle a small amount of nuts in a skillet. It is not necessary to use any oil as the oil in the nuts is sufficient. Cook over medium heat until the nuts are golden brown, stirring frequently. Remove just before the nuts seem to reach the desired colour, keeping in mind that many nuts will continue to toast after being removed from the heat. Transfer the nuts immediately to a plate and allow to cool before serving. Toasted nuts may be stored in an airtight container at room temperature for up to 4 days.

Roasted Portuguese Sausage
and Root Vegetables

4 to 6 red skin potatoes
2 to 4 sweet potatoes
1 large red or yellow yam
4 carrots
1/2 turnip
1 small piece pumpkin
1 red onion
2 Bermuda onions
1/4 cup olive oil
3 or 4 garlic cloves, chopped
1 tablespoon paprika
pinch of fresh thyme
salt and pepper to taste
2 Portuguese chorizo, cut into pieces

Peel the potatoes, sweet potatoes, yam, carrots and turnip or scrub and leave the skins if preferred. Cut into large even chunks. Chop the pumpkin, red onion and Bermuda onions. Combine the vegetables with the olive oil, garlic, paprika, thyme, salt and pepper in a large bowl and mix to coat evenly.

Oil a roasting pan and place in a 350-degree oven to heat. Add the vegetables and sausage to the pan. Roast for 1 hour or until cooked through, stirring occasionally.

Serves 6

Tammy Gibbons

Cassoulet

1 pound boneless chicken
1 pound kielbasa
1 pound ham
vegetable oil
1 large onion, chopped
4 garlic cloves, chopped
6 carrots, sliced and parboiled
2 (16-ounce) cans small red beans, rinsed and drained
1 (16-ounce) can small white beans, rinsed and drained
1 (32-ounce) can whole tomatoes
3 bay leaves
1 tablespoon chili powder
1 teaspoon thyme
1 teaspoon marjoram
1/2 teaspoon salt
pepper to taste

Slice the chicken, kielbasa and ham into 1-inch pieces. Sauté in a small amount of oil in a skillet until light brown. Add the onion and garlic and sauté until tender.

Combine with the carrots, beans, undrained tomatoes, bay leaves, chili powder, thyme, marjoram, salt and pepper in a large baking dish with a lid; mix well.

Bake, covered, at 350 degrees for 45 to 60 minutes or until done to taste, stirring occasionally. Remove the bay leaves and serve with rice, a salad and bread.

You may also prepare this dish in a slow cooker.

Serves 8

Diane Steiger

Golfer's Stew

1¹/₂ pounds stew beef
1 onion, chopped
4 carrots, sliced
4 potatoes, sliced
¹/₂ teaspoon salt
¹/₂ teaspoon lemon pepper
1 teaspoon sugar
1 tablespoon cornstarch
1¹/₂ cups vegetable juice cocktail

Cut the stew beef into small pieces, discarding the fat. Layer the beef, onion, carrots and potatoes in a baking dish. Sprinkle with the salt, lemon pepper, sugar and cornstarch. Pour the vegetable juice cocktail over the layers. Bake, covered with foil, at 250 degrees for 4 hours.

Serves 6

Kelly Marshall

SENIOR CITIZEN'S TEA *For many years, BJSL served tea to senior citizens at an annual tea held in their honour at Camden House, the official residence of the Premier.*

Chicken Vegetable Stir-Fry

1 teaspoon cornstarch
1 teaspoon salt
1 teaspoon light soy sauce
1 pound boneless chicken or pork
  loin, sliced into thin strips
2 tablespoons vegetable oil
4 scallions, sliced diagonally
2 teaspoons finely chopped garlic

1/2 red bell pepper, thinly sliced
1 carrot, thinly sliced
2 cups snow peas
1/2 cup sliced water chestnuts
2 tablespoons white wine
2 tablespoons dark soy sauce
2 teaspoons sugar

Blend the cornstarch and salt with the light soy sauce in a bowl. Add the chicken and toss to coat well. Marinate, covered, in the refrigerator for 30 minutes or longer.

Heat the oil in a wok, swirling to coat the side. Add the scallions and garlic and stir-fry until tender. Add the chicken and stir-fry until opaque and no longer pink. Add the bell pepper, carrot, snow peas and water chestnuts and stir-fry until tender-crisp.

Mix the wine, dark soy sauce and sugar in a small bowl. Add to the wok and cook until heated through. Serve with rice or noodles.

Serves 4   *Elizabeth Zalinger*

Chicken Breasts Supreme

1 (10-ounce) can cream of chicken soup
4 ounces fresh mushrooms, thinly sliced
1/2 cup white wine

1 pound boneless skinless chicken breasts
8 ounces shredded mozzarella cheese
1/4 cup seasoned bread crumbs

Mix the cream of chicken soup, mushrooms and wine in a small bowl. Arrange the chicken in a baking dish and pour the soup mixture over the top. Sprinkle with the mozzarella cheese and bread crumbs. Bake at 350 degrees for 1 hour. Serve with wild rice and green beans topped with toasted almonds.

Serves 4

Pamela Shaw

Chicken Italiano

3/4 cup Italian bread crumbs
3/4 cup (3 ounces) grated Parmesan cheese
1/4 teaspoon paprika
2 eggs, lightly beaten
8 boneless skinless chicken breasts

1/3 cup butter
6 ounces mozzarella cheese, cut into 8 slices
1 (8-ounce) can tomato sauce
parsley

Mix the bread crumbs with the Parmesan cheese and paprika. Dip the chicken breasts into the lightly beaten eggs and coat with the bread crumb mixture. Sauté in the butter in a skillet until light brown on both sides.

Remove to a baking dish and top with the mozzarella cheese. Spoon the tomato sauce over the top and cover tightly with foil. Bake at 350 degrees for 45 minutes. Garnish with parsley.

Serves 8

Kelly Marshall

Chicken with Orange Sauce

1/4 cup (1/2 stick) butter
4 chicken breasts
2 tablespoons Cointreau or orange juice
1/2 cup orange juice
1 cup water
1 small cube chicken bouillon
1 tablespoon honey
green onions, chopped
1 tablespoon grated orange zest
1 tablespoon corn flour

Heat the butter in a skillet and add the chicken. Sauté for 5 minutes or until light brown on both sides and cooked through. Remove the chicken to a serving dish and keep warm.

Stir the liqueur, orange juice, 1 cup water, chicken bouillon, honey, green onions and orange zest into the skillet and bring to a boil. Reduce the heat.

Blend the corn flour with enough water to make a thin paste in a small bowl. Add to the skillet and cook until the mixture thickens, stirring constantly. Pour over the chicken. Serve over rice.

Serves 4   Paula Dilney-Friend

INDIVIDUAL ASSISTANCE BJSL provides funds to aid individuals in need of items such as wheel chairs, hearing aids, and physical therapy.

Chicken and Pasta in Vodka Sauce

VODKA SAUCE

1 small onion, minced
3 garlic cloves, crushed
2 (8-ounce) cans plum tomatoes
pinch of oregano
1 teaspoon pepper
2 cups (1 pint) heavy cream
1/2 cup (4 ounces) vodka

CHICKEN AND PASTA

16 ounces uncooked penne
1 pound chicken tenders
salt and pepper to taste

For the sauce, sauté the onion and garlic in a nonstick saucepan until tender. Add the tomatoes, oregano and pepper; mix well. Simmer for 10 to 15 minutes. Stir in the cream and vodka.

For the chicken and pasta, cook the penne using the package directions; drain and keep warm. Season the chicken with salt and pepper. Sauté in a skillet until light brown and cooked through.

To serve, heat the sauce just to serving temperature. Spoon the pasta onto serving plates. Arrange the chicken over the pasta and spoon the sauce over the top.

Serves 4

Kim Moseley

Chicken and Shrimp Fettuccini

1 large whole boneless chicken breast
8 ounces uncooked shrimp, peeled and deveined
2 tablespoons dry sherry
1 tablespoon cornstarch
1 teaspoon grated gingerroot, or $1/4$ teaspoon ground ginger
12 ounces uncooked fettuccini
2 tablespoons vegetable oil
16 ounces small mushrooms or large mushrooms cut into quarters
3 tablespoons soy sauce
$1/4$ cup vegetable oil
8 ounces spinach, coarsely chopped
red bell pepper strips

Cut the chicken breast into halves crosswise and cut the halves into $1/2$-inch strips. Toss the chicken and shrimp with the sherry, cornstarch and gingerroot in a bowl. Cook the fettuccini using the package directions, drain and keep warm.

Heat 2 tablespoons oil in a 2-quart saucepan over high heat. Add the mushrooms and soy sauce and cook for several minutes. Reduce the heat and simmer for 5 minutes.

Heat $1/4$ cup oil in a 4-quart saucepan. Add the chicken mixture and sauté until cooked through.

Spoon the pasta onto a platter. Sprinkle with the spinach and spoon the chicken mixture over the top. Spoon the mushrooms over the chicken mixture and garnish with bell pepper. Toss to serve.

Serves 4

Greta Carne

Turkey Chili

2 tablespoons olive oil
1 large onion, thinly sliced
1 green or red bell pepper, chopped
2 garlic cloves, minced
1^1/$_2$ pounds chopped cooked turkey breast
2 (14-ounce) cans chicken broth
1 cup medium salsa
^{3}/$_4$ cup uncooked rice
1 (4-ounce) can chopped green chiles
2 tablespoons chili powder
2 teaspoons ground cumin
^{1}/$_2$ teaspoon salt
^{1}/$_2$ teaspoon pepper
1 (16-ounce) can cannellini beans
1 (16-ounce) can black beans
1 (10-ounce) package frozen corn

Heat the olive oil in a large saucepan and add the onion, bell pepper and garlic; sauté until the onion is translucent. Add the turkey, chicken broth, salsa, rice, green chiles, chili powder, cumin, salt and pepper and mix well. Simmer for 15 minutes.

Rinse and drain the cannellini beans and black beans. Add to the chili with the corn and mix well. Simmer for 15 minutes longer or until the rice is tender. Serve with sour cream, tortilla chips and lime wedges.

You can make the chili milder by using a mild salsa, reducing the amount of chili powder and omitting the green chiles.

Serves 8

Diane Steiger

Spicy Vegetarian Chili

1 tablespoon olive oil
1 large onion, chopped
1 green bell pepper, chopped
2 garlic cloves, chopped
1½ tablespoons chili powder
½ teaspoon cumin
¼ teaspoon cayenne pepper
2 cups chopped fresh tomatoes or drained canned tomatoes
3 cups cooked red kidney beans
1 cup chopped zucchini
1 cup canned corn

Heat the olive oil in a saucepan. Add the onion, bell pepper and garlic and sauté for 5 minutes. Add the chili powder, cumin and cayenne pepper and sauté for 30 seconds.

Stir in the tomatoes, beans, zucchini and corn. Bring to a boil and reduce the heat. Simmer, covered, over low heat for 20 to 30 minutes or to the desired consistency. Serve with Tropical Salsa (page 172) if desired.

Serves 6   *Wendy Railton*

Easy Burritos

1 (15-ounce) can black beans
4 (10-inch) flour tortillas
2 cups warm cooked brown rice
1 cup (4 ounces) shredded Cheddar cheese
2 cups shredded lettuce
1 avocado, chopped
2 vine-ripened tomatoes, chopped
Tropical Salsa (below)

Heat the beans in a saucepan until warm.
Warm the tortillas using the package
directions. Layer the rice, beans, cheese,
lettuce, avocado and tomatoes on
the tortillas and roll to enclose the filing.
Serve with Tropical Salsa.

Serves 4   *Nikki Blagden*

Tropical Salsa

1 1/2 cups chopped mango
1 1/2 cups chopped paw paw
1 cup chopped tomato
1 cup chopped red bell pepper

1/4 cup chopped coriander leaves
3 tablespoons canola oil
2 tablespoons white wine vinegar
salt to taste

Combine the mango, paw paw, tomato, bell pepper and coriander leaves in a bowl and mix well. Stir in the
canola oil, white wine vinegar and salt. Chill for 1 hour or longer. Serve with burritos, chili or fish or with chips
as an appetizer.

Makes 4 cups

Penne Gorgonzola

1 cup (8 ounces) cream
2 tablespoons butter
4 ounces gorgonzola, dolcelatte or other blue-veined cheese, crumbled
salt and pepper to taste
1 cup uncooked penne

Combine the cream and butter in a small saucepan over low to medium heat and cook until the butter melts, stirring to blend well. Add the cheese. Cook until the cheese melts and the mixture is thickened and slightly reduced, stirring constantly. Season with salt and pepper.

Cook the pasta using the package directions; drain well. Combine with the sauce in a bowl and toss to coat well. Serve immediately.

Serves 2   *Susan Patton*

Summer Spaghetti Sauce

2 garlic cloves, chopped
pinch of marjoram
pinch of thyme
2 tablespoons olive oil
1 (28-ounce) can whole plum tomatoes
10 ounces spinach, coarsely torn
grated Parmesan cheese to taste

Stir the garlic, marjoram and thyme into the olive oil in a saucepan and cook over low heat for 30 minutes, stirring to avoid overbrowning. Add the undrained tomatoes and crush against the side of the saucepan. Cook for 10 minutes.

Add the spinach and cook, covered, for several minutes; mix well. Serve over cooked spaghetti. Sprinkle with Parmesan cheese if desired.

Serves 4   *Sally Gibbons*

On The Side

Baked Beans

1 large onion, chopped
4 slices bacon, chopped
1 pound dried navy beans or lima beans
6 cups water
1/2 to 1 cup molasses
salt to taste

Sauté the onion with the bacon in a skillet until the bacon is brown and the onion is tender. Combine with the beans and water in a slow cooker. Stir in the molasses and season with salt. Cook on Low for 4 to 5 hours or until the beans are tender, adding additional water if needed.

Serves 8   *Susan Titterton*

Almond and Broccoli Casserole

1/2 cup chopped celery
1/2 cup chopped onion
1/4 cup (1/2 stick) margarine
1/2 roll garlic cheese
1 cup sliced mushrooms
1 (10-ounce) can cream of mushroom soup
1 tablespoon lemon juice
1 tablespoon Worcestershire sauce
ground red pepper to taste
2 (10-ounce) packages frozen broccoli, cooked and drained
slivered almonds

Sauté the celery and onion in the margarine in a saucepan. Add the garlic cheese, mushrooms, soup, lemon juice, Worcestershire sauce and red pepper. Cook until the cheese melts, stirring to mix well.

Place the broccoli in a buttered baking dish. Spoon the cheese sauce over the top and sprinkle with almonds. Bake at 350 degrees until heated through.

Serves 8   *Wendi Ryland*

Marsala Carrots

6 large carrots, julienned
1/4 cup marsala
1 tablespoon olive oil
salt and pepper to taste

Parboil the carrots in water in a saucepan for 5 minutes; drain the carrots and return to the saucepan. Add the wine and olive oil and simmer, covered, until the carrots are tender-crisp. Season with salt and pepper. Serve immediately or store in the refrigerator for up to 24 hours. You may serve this Sicilian dish cold if preferred.

Serves 4 to 6

Rosalind Gutteridge

Pickled Mushrooms

1 cup cider vinegar
1 cup packed light brown sugar
1/2 cup water
2 tablespoons pickling spice
1 pound fresh mushrooms, sliced

Combine the cider vinegar, brown sugar, water and pickling spice in a saucepan. Bring to a boil and reduce the heat. Simmer for 5 minutes. Pour over the mushrooms in a bowl. Cover and let stand until cool. Store in the refrigerator.

You may also serve this as an appetizer.

Serves 6

Mary Lou Trimingham

BERMUDA ONIONS

English onions were introduced to Bermuda around 1616. Approximately 215 years later, they became a major export to the USA. Its success led to Bermudians being known as "Onions" and Bermuda as "The Onion Patch." Texans later developed the Bermudian onion seed and grew it for domestic distribution, making it no longer cost effective for Bermuda to export.

BERMUDA HONEY

Bees were first imported to Bermuda on a British ship in 1616. Bermuda honey has a unique, strong flavour attributed to the fact that the bees are free to roam and extract nectar from a wide variety of blossoms.

Onions in Cream Sauce

4 large onions, cut into quarters
3 to 4 tablespoons water
1/2 cup (1 stick) butter
1/4 cup flour
1 teaspoon salt
2 1/2 cups milk

Place the onions in a microwave-safe bowl and add the water. Cover with plastic wrap and microwave on High for 5 to 8 minutes or until tender; drain.

Melt the butter in a microwave-safe bowl. Stir in the flour and salt until smooth. Add the milk gradually. Microwave until thickened, stirring frequently. Combine with the onions in a baking dish. Bake at 350 degrees until heated through.

Serves 6   *Kim Paterson*

Honeyed Onions

1 pound small Bermuda onions
1/4 cup Bermuda honey
1/4 cup black rum
3 tablespoons butter

Cook the onions in enough water to cover in a large saucepan until fork tender. Combine the honey, rum and butter in a large skillet. Cook over low heat until the butter melts, stirring to mix well. Drain the onions and add to the skillet. Cook until the onions are glazed, stirring frequently; reduce the heat to very low if necessary to prevent overbrowning.

Serves 6   *Elizabeth Zalinger*

Paw Paw Montespan

3 small green paw paws
4 ounces ground round
1 small chorizo, chopped
2 medium onions, chopped
salt and pepper to taste

1 (10-ounce) can tomato soup
1 cup (4 ounces) shredded cheese
1 package seasoned bread crumbs
butter

Peel and chop the paw paws, discarding the seeds. Cook in enough water to cover in a saucepan until tender; drain and mash the paw paws. Sauté the ground round and chorizo with the onions, salt and pepper in a nonstick skillet until the meats are cooked through.

Layer the paw paw mixture, soup, ground round mixture and cheese 1/2 at a time in a baking dish. Top with the bread crumbs and dot with butter. Place in a larger pan and add enough water to reach halfway up the side of the baking dish. Bake at 350 degrees for 40 to 60 minutes or until heated through.

Serves 6   *Dawn Dunstan*

Parisian Potatoes

6 medium potatoes, peeled
1 tablespoon butter

garlic powder and paprika to taste
seasoning salt and pepper to taste

Scoop the potatoes into small balls with a melon baller. Add to boiling water in a saucepan and return to a full boil. Remove from the heat and drain; cool to room temperature.

Sauté the potatoes in the butter in a skillet until the potatoes are tender but still hold their shape, sprinkling with the garlic powder, paprika, seasoning salt and pepper. Serve hot.

Serves 6   *Dawn Dunstan*

PAW PAWS

More commonly known in North America as the papaya, the paw paw is a very different fruit than the papaw, which resembles a large dark brown banana and is seldom cultivated. The seed of the paw paw grows to a twenty-foot tree and bears fruit in less than eighteen months. The flesh is bright orange or pinkish, depending on the variety, with small black seeds reminiscent of black pepper in flavour. A properly ripened paw paw is juicy, sweet, and similar to a cantaloupe in flavour. Bermudians use paw paw as a vegetable when green and a fruit when fully ripe.

Cassava Pie

8 pounds cassava, grated
4 pounds chicken breasts
4 pounds chicken thighs
thyme to taste
salt to taste
2 pounds pork
1¹/₂ pounds (6 sticks) butter

2 cups sugar
24 eggs
¹/₂ cup flour
2 teaspoons (heaping) baking
  powder
rum to taste
sugar and nutmeg to taste

Tie the cassava in a cheesecloth bag. Squeeze to remove excess moisture and allow to drain for 8 hours or longer. Combine the chicken with enough water to cover, thyme and salt in a large saucepan. Cook for 1 hour or until tender; drain, reserving the stock. Chill the chicken stock; remove and reserve the fat. Cook the pork in enough water to cover in a saucepan until tender; drain. Chop the chicken and pork, discarding any skin and bones.

Cream the butter and 2 cups sugar in a large mixing bowl until light and fluffy. Beat in the eggs and reserved fat from the chicken stock. Add the cassava and mix well. Beat in the flour and baking powder and season with rum, additional sugar, nutmeg and salt.

Layer half the cassava mixture in 5 greased loaf pans or a 12×16-inch baking pan. Spread the chicken and pork over the cassava layer and top with the remaining cassava mixture; press down to compact. Poke 2 rows of holes in the pie to aid with basting. Bake at 240 degrees for 3 to 4 hours or until done to taste, basting with the reserved chicken stock.

For a lighter version of this dish, substitute 3 cups of egg substitute for the eggs and substitute 12 ounces of margarine for 12 ounces of the butter.

Serves 24

Carolyn Toogood

Sweet Potato Pie Casserole

SWEET POTATOES

3 or 4 sweet potatoes
1 (14-ounce) can sweetened condensed milk
1/2 cup (1 stick) butter
3/4 to 1 cup sugar
1 teaspoon vanilla extract
1 tablespoon nutmeg, or to taste
1 tablespoon cinnamon, or to taste

PECAN TOPPING

1/2 cup (1 stick) butter
3/4 cup packed brown sugar
1 cup corn flakes
1/2 cup pecans

For the sweet potatoes, peel and slice the sweet potatoes. Combine with enough water to cover in a saucepan and cook until fork tender; drain. Add the sweetened condensed milk, butter, sugar, vanilla, nutmeg and cinnamon and mash until smooth. Adjust the sugar and seasonings. Spoon into a baking dish. Bake at 350 degrees for 20 minutes.

For the topping, melt the butter with the brown sugar in a saucepan and mix well. Stir in the corn flakes and pecans. Spread over the sweet potatoes. Bake for 20 minutes longer, covering with foil if necessary to keep the pecans from overbrowning.

Serves 6 to 10

Mollie Meyer

Creamed Spinach with Garlic

9 ounces fresh spinach
$1/4$ cup ($1/2$ stick) butter
3 garlic cloves, crushed or chopped
1 tablespoon flour
salt and pepper to taste
$1/4$ cup milk

Steam the spinach over boiling water in a saucepan for 4 minutes; drain the spinach in the steamer rack. Pour the water from the saucepan.

Melt the butter in the saucepan and add the garlic; sauté until tender. Stir in the flour, salt and pepper. Add the milk and cook until the mixture is thickened and smooth, stirring constantly. Add the spinach and mix gently. Serve with fish or use as a stuffing for mushrooms.

Serves 4 to 6

Rosalind Gutteridge

Roasted Summer Vegetables

3 medium zucchini
4 medium red potatoes
1 large red bell pepper
1 large yellow bell pepper
1 large orange bell pepper
1 large onion
3 garlic cloves, finely chopped
1/4 cup chopped fresh parsley
1 teaspoon dried oregano
1 teaspoon dried marjoram
1/2 teaspoon dried thyme
salt and pepper to taste
olive oil
red wine vinegar or balsamic vinegar

Cut the zucchini, potatoes, bell peppers and onion into chunks. Combine with the garlic and parsley in a roasting pan. Add the oregano, marjoram, thyme, salt and pepper. Drizzle with enough olive oil to coat and toss to coat evenly. Press down lightly.

Roast at 350 degrees for 45 minutes or until the vegetables are fork tender and the edges are brown. Sprinkle with vinegar and serve warm or at room temperature. This dish forms the base of the Flank Steak Salad on page 140.

Serves 6

Sally Gibbons

THYME

Thyme is one of the most versatile herbs for the home kitchen. A perennial herb, thyme is widely used to flavour meats, poultry, fish, and soups. Thyme needs to be added early in the cooking process to allow the oils and the flavour to release. Fresh thyme can be used whole as a sprig and removed before serving or by stripping the leaves and adding them directly to the ingredients.

Thyme grows as a bush with a warm, pungent mint and lemon aroma. When grown in dry conditions, the plant develops as a shrubby, woodsy plant and tends to concentrate the oils, producing a more potent herb. Well-watered thyme becomes supple and lush with densely spaced leaves. Thyme can be planted during any season and needs about 6 hours of direct sunlight daily.

Chestnut Stuffing

2 (10-ounce) cans or jars chestnuts in water
6 tablespoons (3/4 stick) butter, melted
1 tablespoon sugar, or to taste
salt and pepper to taste

Drain the chestnuts; mash with a pastry blender in a bowl until smooth. Add the melted butter, sugar, salt and pepper and mix well.

Spoon into the neck cavity of a turkey and bake with the turkey or spoon into a baking dish and bake at 350 degrees until heated through. Serve warm with a turkey dinner.

Serves 4

Dawn Dunstan

PATIENT SUPPLIES *Each month, BJSL members provide supplies, such as magazines and toiletries, for patients and residents of St. Brendan's Hospital and the King Edward VII Memorial Hospital's Extended Care Unit..*

Bacon and Spinach Stuffing

1 pound sliced bacon
3 cups coarsely chopped onions
3 ribs celery, sliced $1/2$ inch thick
1 teaspoon salt
1 teaspoon pepper
3 large garlic cloves, minced
15 ounces baby spinach leaves, coarsely chopped
1 thick country-style loaf of bread, cut into $1/2$-inch cubes and lightly toasted
2 cups salted cashews, coarsely chopped
$1/2$ cup (1 stick) unsalted butter
1 cup turkey broth or chicken broth

Cut the bacon into $1/2$-inch pieces. Fry in a large skillet for 10 minutes or until crisp; remove to a plate lined with paper towels and pat to drain well.

Pour all but $1/3$ cup of the bacon drippings from the skillet. Add the onions, celery, salt and pepper to the drippings in the skillet and sauté for 5 minutes or until the vegetables are tender. Add the garlic and sauté for 1 minute longer.

Combine with the spinach, bread cubes, cashews, butter, bacon and turkey broth in a bowl; mix well. Cool completely and serve at room temperature.

Serves 8

Carolyn Toogood

Macaroni and Cheese Casserole

16 ounces uncooked macaroni
8 ounces cottage cheese
1 cup (4 ounces) shredded Cheddar cheese

1 small onion, finely chopped
salt and pepper to taste
parsley and paprika to taste

Cook the macaroni using the package directions; drain. Combine the macaroni with the cottage cheese, Cheddar cheese and onion in a bowl. Season with salt and pepper.

Spoon into a baking dish and bake at 350 degrees for 30 minutes. Top with parsley and paprika.

You may top with bread crumbs and additional Cheddar cheese before baking if desired.

Serves 8

Mrs. C. Vail Zuill, MBE
Janette R. Zuill, Founding President

Hoppin' John

1½ cups dried black-eyed peas or red beans
chopped onion to taste
thyme and salt to taste
1 cup uncooked rice

1 vegetable bouillon cube
2 cups coconut juice or coconut water
1 tablespoon butter
bell pepper rings

Combine the peas with onion, thyme, salt and enough water to cover in an ovenproof dish. Cook over medium heat until the peas are partially cooked. Stir in the rice, vegetable bouillon cube, coconut juice and butter. Bake, covered, at 250 degrees for 20 minutes or until golden brown. Garnish with bell pepper rings.

Serves 10

Melanie Whaley

Peanut Rice

1 tablespoon olive oil
3 whole garlic cloves
2 teaspoons cumin seeds
1 bay leaf
$1/8$ teaspoon allspice
$1/4$ teaspoon red pepper
3 scallions, finely chopped
1 cup uncooked organic jasmine rice
2 cups chicken broth
$1/2$ teaspoon salt
$1/3$ cup chopped peanuts

Heat the olive oil in a saucepan. Add the garlic, cumin seeds, bay leaf and allspice and cook for 5 to 10 minutes or until aromatic. Remove the garlic with a slotted spoon and add the red pepper, scallions and rice, stirring to coat well. Stir in the chicken broth and salt. Bring to a boil and reduce the heat. Simmer, covered, for 50 minutes.

Remove from the heat and let stand for 10 minutes; discard the bay leaf. Fluff with a fork and stir in the peanuts to serve.

Serves 4 to 6

Julia Bolton

Risi and Bisi

6 cups chicken stock
2 tablespoons olive oil
$^1/_4$ cup chopped onion
$^1/_2$ cup chopped parsley
1 cup uncooked arborio rice
1 (10-ounce) package frozen peas
3 tablespoons grated Parmesan cheese
1 teaspoon salt, or to taste
freshly ground pepper to taste

Bring the chicken stock to a simmer in a saucepan over medium heat. Reduce the heat and keep the stock hot.

Heat the olive oil in a heavy saucepan and add the onion and parsley. Sauté for 3 minutes or until the onion is tender but not brown. Add 1$^1/_2$ cups of the stock and bring to a boil. Stir in the rice and reduce the heat to medium. Simmer until the liquid is absorbed, adding additional stock $^1/_2$ cup at a time and stirring constantly after each addition; the process should take about 20 minutes.

Stir in the peas and cook for 1 minute. Add the Parmesan cheese, salt and pepper. Simmer for 2 minutes. Serve with a green salad and hearty bread.

Serves 4

Susan Behrens

Spiced Pumpkin Rice

1 (4×6-inch) piece of fresh pumpkin, or 2 cups chopped pumpkin
1 (14-ounce) can coconut milk
1 vegetable bouillon cube
1 large onion, chopped
3 large garlic cloves, chopped
4 ribs celery, chopped
1 (1-inch) piece gingerroot, grated
2 tablespoons olive oil

1¹/₂ cups uncooked rice
1 tablespoon butter
¹/₂ teaspoon ground cumin
¹/₂ teaspoon ground coriander
¹/₂ teaspoon turmeric
thyme to taste
1 bay leaf
celery salt, salt and pepper to taste
1 tablespoon butter

Cut the pumpkin into very small pieces. Pour the coconut milk into a large measuring cup. Add enough water to measure 3 cups. Combine with the vegetable bouillon cube in a saucepan and bring to a boil. Reduce the heat and keep warm.

Sauté the pumpkin, onion, garlic, celery and gingerroot in olive oil in a heavy saucepan until the onion is tender. Add the rice, 1 tablespoon butter, cumin, coriander, turmeric, thyme, bay leaf, celery salt, salt and pepper. Cook over low heat for 2 minutes, stirring to coat the rice well.

Add the heated coconut milk mixture. Cook for 5 minutes. Spoon into a baking dish and bake at 350 degrees for 30 minutes or until the rice is tender. Stir and add 1 tablespoon butter and additional celery salt; discard the bay leaf.

You may substitute 2 tablespoons curry powder for the cumin, coriander and turmeric. To avoid soggy rice, place a dish towel over the saucepan after the water comes to a boil and place the lid over it. The towel will absorb moisture buildup from the steam, and the water will not drip down onto the rice.

Serves 6   *Tammy Gibbons*

Wild Rice with Chives

1 cup uncooked wild rice
1/2 cup (1 stick) butter or margarine
salt to taste
1/2 cup slivered almonds
2 tablespoons thinly sliced chives or green onions
1 (8-ounce) can mushrooms, drained
3 cups chicken broth

Rinse and drain the rice. Melt the butter in a large skillet. Add the rice, almonds, chives and mushrooms. Sauté for 20 minutes or until the almonds are golden brown. Spoon into an ungreased 1 1/2-quart baking dish.

Bring the chicken broth to a boil in a saucepan. Pour over the rice. Cover the dish tightly and bake at 325 degrees for 1 1/2 hours or until the liquid is absorbed. Serve with poultry, fish or meat dishes.

You may use canned chicken broth in this recipe or dissolve 3 chicken bouillon cubes in 3 cups boiling water if preferred.

Serves 6 to 8

Mollie Meyer

DELIVERANCE *BJSL built a replica of the Deliverance, the first ship built in Bermuda, which took supplies to the starving colony of Jamestown in 1610. The Deliverance admission profits were donated to many charities. BJSL operated it until 1995, when it was sold for $70,000 and the proceeds purchased the playground at WindReach Recreational Village.*

Measure an equal amount of sugar for the stoned cherries to be used. Alternate layers of cherries and sugar in a large bowl. Let stand, covered with a towel, for 8 hours or longer. Pour into a saucepan and bring to a boil, stirring constantly. Reduce the heat and simmer until thickened, stirring frequently. Pour into sterilised jars and seal.

Banana Chutney

2 medium onions, finely chopped	1 1/2 cups vinegar
2 tablespoons butter or margarine	2/3 cup sugar
6 bananas, mashed	6 whole cloves
2/3 cup raisins	1 (2-inch) cinnamon stick
2 cups water	1 teaspoon ginger

Sauté the onions in the butter in a skillet. Combine with the bananas, raisins, water, vinegar and sugar in a saucepan. Tie the cloves, cinnamon and ginger in a cheesecloth bag and add to the saucepan.

Simmer for 20 minutes or until the mixture thickens to the desired consistency, stirring frequently. Remove the spices. Pour into sterilised jelly glasses and seal.

To sterilise jars and jelly glasses, wash well with hot water. Place on a baking sheet and place in a 200-degree oven for 30 minutes. Cool and place on a wet cloth to prevent cracking when the hot fruit is added.

Makes 4 (8-ounce) glasses   *Louise Gibbons*

Loquat Chutney

1¹/₂ to 2 pounds loquats
1 apple, chopped
1 onion, chopped
1 red bell pepper, chopped
1 cup seedless raisins
1 ounce gingerroot, peeled and
  chopped

2 cups vinegar
2 cups packed brown sugar
1 teaspoon curry powder
1 teaspoon allspice
1 teaspoon nutmeg
1 teaspoon salt

Cut the loquats into small pieces, discarding the seeds. Combine the loquats, apple, onion, bell pepper, raisins and gingerroot in a saucepan. Add the vinegar, brown sugar, curry powder, allspice, nutmeg and salt and mix well. Cook over low heat for 1 hour or until the fruit is tender and the mixture is thick, stirring frequently. Spoon into sterilised jars and seal.

Makes 6 (6-ounce) jars   *Susan Smith*

Loquat Jam

6 cups seeded loquat quarters
seeds from 6 cups loquat quarters
1 cup water

4 cups sugar
1 ounce green gingerroot, peeled
  and grated

Cut the loquats into quarters, reserving the seeds. Measure 6 cups loquats. Tie the loquat seeds in a muslin bag and combine with the loquats and water in a saucepan. Cook until tender. Discard the bag of seeds and add the sugar and gingerroot. Cook until thickened, stirring occasionally. Spoon into sterilised jars and seal.

Makes 6 (6-ounce) jars   *Susan Smith*

BAY GRAPE JELLY

Combine an equal amount of green and ripe bay grapes in a large skillet and add enough water to cover. Cook until tender. Mash and strain through cheesecloth, reserving the juice. Measure the juice and combine with 1 cup of sugar for every cup of juice in a saucepan. Bring to a boil and cook for 20 minutes, skimming the surface. Pour into sterilised jars and seal.

The bay grape tree and shrub grow on Bermuda's rocky coastline, being able to easily withstand sea spray and salty soil conditions. The shiny bright green leaves are leathery and veined in red. Bermudians often use them in holiday decorations.

NATAL
PLUM JELLY

Combine the Natal plums with just enough water to cover in a saucepan. Simmer until tender. Mash the plums and strain through a cheesecloth or fine mesh strainer, reserving the juice. Measure the juice and return to the saucepan. Add 1 cup of sugar for each cup of juice. Simmer for 30 minutes or until thickened. Spoon into sterilised jars and seal.

The Natal plum is an edible fruit that grows on a waxy-leafed tropical garden shrub. It easily withstands the wind and salt and produces white star-like flowers that are especially fragrant at night. The fruit is a plum-shaped red berry 2 inches in diameter that tastes like sweet cranberries and makes wonderful jam or jelly.

Cranberry Relish

1/2 cup orange juice
2 cups sugar
1 Granny Smith apple, peeled and cut into wedges
1 (12-ounce) package cranberries
1/4 cup grated orange zest

Combine the orange juice and sugar in a food processor and process for 1 to 2 minutes. Add the apple and pulse until the apple is chopped. Add the cranberries and pulse until the cranberries are minced. Stir in the orange zest. Store in covered jars in the refrigerator.

Makes 2 (12-ounce) jars   Cornelia Kempe

Mustard Sauce for Ham

1/2 cup dry mustard
1/2 cup white vinegar
1 egg
1/3 cup sugar
salt to taste
1 1/4 cups (about) mayonnaise

Mix the dry mustard with the white vinegar in a jar. Cover and let stand for 8 hours or longer. Beat the egg in a saucepan and stir in the sugar, salt and mustard mixture. Cook over low heat until the mixture thickens enough to coat the spoon, stirring constantly. Let stand until cool. Mix with an equal amount of mayonnaise in a bowl. Store in the refrigerator. Serve with ham.

Makes 2 1/2 cups

Sue Sharpe

Spiced Raisin Sauce for Ham

1/2 cup sugar
1 tablespoon cornstarch
1 cup water
1/4 cup white vinegar
1 cup raisins
1/2 teaspoon allspice
salt to taste

Mix the sugar and cornstarch in a saucepan. Add the water and white vinegar and mix until smooth. Stir in the raisins, allspice and salt. Cook for 5 minutes or until thickened and clear, stirring constantly. Serve with ham.

Makes about 2 cups

Sue Sharpe

Desserts

Apple Dumplings

DUMPLING SAUCE

2 cups sugar
2 cups water
1/4 cup (1/2 stick) margarine or butter
1/4 teaspoon ground cinnamon
1/4 teaspoon ground nutmeg

DUMPLING PASTRY

2 cups flour
2 teaspoons baking powder
1/2 teaspoon salt
3/4 cup shortening
2/3 cup milk

APPLE FILLING

1/4 cup sugar
1/2 teaspoon ground cinnamon
3 cups peeled and sliced McIntosh apples,
   about 4 to 6 apples

For the sauce, mix the sugar, water, margarine, cinnamon and nutmeg in a saucepan and bring to a boil. Cook for 3 to 5 minutes or until the sugar is dissolved and the mixture is thickened and smooth, stirring frequently.

For the pastry, mix the flour, baking powder and salt in a bowl. Cut in the shortening with a pastry blender. Make a well in the center and add the milk, mixing to form a dough. Knead until smooth on a floured surface. Roll into a rectangle 12 inches long.

For the filling, mix the sugar and cinnamon in a small bowl. Arrange the apples evenly over the dough and sprinkle with the cinnamon-sugar. Roll the dough from the long side to enclose the filling; press the edges to seal. Cut into twelve 1-inch pieces and arrange in a 9x13-inch baking pan.

Spoon the sauce over the dumplings. Bake at 350 degrees for 50 minutes or until golden brown.

Makes 1 dozen

Kendra Wharton

Flaming Surinam Cherries

¹/₄ cup (¹/₂ stick) butter
1 cup pitted Surinam cherries
¹/₄ cup sugar
¹/₄ cup white rum
4 servings vanilla ice cream

Melt the butter in a small saucepan. Add the Surinam cherries and sugar.
Cook until the sugar dissolves, stirring constantly. Add the rum and cook for
1 minute, stirring constantly. Ignite and allow the flames to subside. Serve over
the ice cream.

Serves 4   *Bermudian Cookery*

SURINAM CHERRIES

The Surinam cherry tree is grown as a hedge in Bermuda, often lining the roadside. The ribbed round fruit is similar in size to a black cherry and becomes bright red to deep scarlet when fully ripe. The juicy flesh is orange-red and has a sweet taste with a touch of resin and a slight bitterness. Children enjoy the ripe fruits right off the tree. For table use, slit them vertically, spread open to remove the seed, sprinkle with sugar and place in the refrigerator, where they will become mild and sweet and exude a large quantity of juice. Surinam cherries can be served in the place of strawberries and topped with whipped cream on shortcake. They are an excellent addition to fruit cups, salads, and custard pudding and are often made into jam, jelly, relish, or pickles.

Bailey's Irish Cream Cheesecake
with Berries

CHEESECAKE

24 ounces cream cheese, softened
1 cup sugar
2 teaspoons vanilla extract
1 cup sour cream
1/3 cup Bailey's Irish Cream
4 eggs

BERRY TOPPING

1 cup sour cream
1/4 cup Bailey's Irish Cream
1/4 cup sugar
2 pints mixed strawberries, raspberries and
    blueberries
1 tablespoon balsamic vinegar
sugar to taste

For the cheesecake, combine the cream cheese, sugar and vanilla in a mixing bowl and beat until smooth. Add the sour cream and Bailey's Irish Cream and mix well. Add the eggs 1 at a time, mixing just until smooth after each addition.

Spoon into a greased springform pan. Bake at 325 degrees for 1 hour or until the edges begin to pull away from the side of the pan. Remove to a wire rack to cool for 15 minutes.

For the topping, mix the sour cream, Bailey's Irish Cream and 1/4 cup sugar in a bowl. Spread over the cheesecake. Bake for 10 minutes longer. Let stand on a wire rack until cool. Chill in the refrigerator. Place on a serving plate and remove the side of the pan. Mix the berries and balsamic vinegar in a bowl and sweeten with sugar to taste. Spoon over the cheesecake at serving time.

Serves 12

Kim Moseley

Grilled Pineapple Dessert

1 pineapple
1 1/2 teaspoons brown sugar
2 tablespoons butter or black rum
vanilla ice cream

Peel the pineapple and cut into quarters; remove the cores. Slice each quarter into halves to yield 8 slices. Mix the brown sugar and butter in a small saucepan and heat until the butter melts and the brown sugar dissolves. Brush over the pineapple.

Grill over medium heat for 4 minutes on each side, turning once. Serve with ice cream.

Serves 8   Deborah Titterton Narraway

GROWING PINEAPPLES

Pineapples do grow in Bermuda, but local conditions are not conducive to growing them in large quantities. You can grow a pineapple, too. The next time you have a pineapple, cut off the top and place it in a pot with a mixture of half soil and half sand; it may root. Keep the soil slightly damp and in a bright location for two months or until roots develop. Then you should see some new growth at the top of the plant. It can then be planted in the ground. Continued care includes high light, constant humidity, and constant light fertilizer in the summertime. In two or three years, it will grow another pineapple.

Chocolate Creams

5 ounces chocolate
10 ounces double cream

1 egg
several drops of vanilla extract

Break the chocolate into pieces and place in a blender. Bring the cream to a boil in a saucepan and pour over the chocolate. Process until the chocolate melts and the mixture is smooth. Add the egg and vanilla and process until smooth. Spoon into small dishes or ramekins. Chill until set or freeze for up to 2 months.

To avoid raw eggs that may carry salmonella, use an equivalent amount of pasteurised egg substitute.

Serves 6

Audrey Smith

Chocolate Crème Brûlée

4 cups heavy cream
1/2 cup sugar
12 ounces chocolate, finely chopped

8 egg yolks
sugar

Bring the cream and 1/2 cup sugar to a simmer in a small saucepan and remove from the heat. Add the chocolate and let stand for 3 minutes; whisk until smooth. Whisk the egg yolks in a mixing bowl. Whisk in the chocolate mixture gradually. Strain through a fine mesh strainer into a bowl. Spoon into 8 ramekins.

Place the ramekins in a baking pan and add enough water to reach halfway up the sides of the ramekins. Bake at 300 degrees for 1 hour. Sprinkle with additional sugar and caramelise with a kitchen torch or place under the broiler until caramelised.

Serves 8

Wendi Ryland

Chilled Chocolate Ladyfinger Dessert

2 packages ladyfingers
2 (3 1/2-ounce) packages chocolate pudding and pie filling mix
2 egg yolks, beaten
1/2 cup sugar
1 cup heavy whipping cream
2 egg whites
1/2 cup finely chopped walnuts
1/4 cup grated white chocolate

Butter the side of a springform pan and sprinkle with sugar. Line the bottom and side with ladyfingers, cutting where necessary to fit the pan. Prepare and cook the chocolate pudding mix using the package directions. Add the egg yolks and sugar and cook over medium heat until thickened, stirring constantly; do not boil. Spoon into a bowl and cool to room temperature.

Whip the cream in a bowl until soft peaks form. Fold into the pudding mixture. Beat the egg whites in a bowl until fluffy. Fold into the pudding mixture with the walnuts. Spoon into the prepared springform pan and sprinkle with the white chocolate. Freeze for 3 hours or longer. Place in the refrigerator until softened enough to cut. Place on a serving plate and remove the side of the pan. Cut into wedges to serve.

Serves 12

Pamela Shaw

Chocolate Mousse

12 ounces semisweet chocolate chips, or
  semisweet chocolate, broken into pieces
3 eggs

1 tablespoon Grand Marnier
1 cup heavy whipping cream
fresh berries

Place the chocolate chips in an ovenproof bowl and place in a 200-degree oven for 4 to 5 minutes or until melted. Cool slightly. Beat the eggs in a medium mixing bowl until foamy. Add to the chocolate mixture gradually, beating constantly at low speed. Add the Grand Marnier and mix well. Beat the whipping cream in a large mixing bowl until soft peaks form. Fold in the chocolate mixture gently. Spoon into I large glass dish or individual stemmed glasses. Chill for 8 hours or longer. Garnish with fresh berries or additional whipped cream.

To avoid raw eggs that may carry salmonella, use an equivalent amount of pasteurised egg substitute.

Serves 6 to 8

Christine Caton

Layered Pudding

WALNUT CRUMB CRUST

1 cup flour
1/2 cup (1 stick) butter, softened
2 tablespoons sugar
1/4 cup walnuts, ground

PUDDING

8 ounces cream cheese, softened
1 cup sugar
8 ounces whipped topping
1 small package vanilla instant pudding mix
1 small package chocolate instant pudding mix
3 cups milk
1 small can walnuts, chopped

For the crumb crust, combine the flour, butter, sugar and ground walnuts in a bowl and mix until crumbly. Press into a 9×13-inch baking dish. Bake at 350 degrees for 15 to 18 minutes or until golden brown. Cool to room temperature.

For the pudding layers, blend the cream cheese and sugar in a mixing bowl until smooth. Fold in half the whipped topping. Spread over the cooled crust and chill in the refrigerator.

Combine the instant pudding mixes with the milk in a bowl and mix until smooth. Spread over the cream cheese layer. Chill in the refrigerator. Spread the remaining whipped topping over the layers and sprinkle with the chopped walnuts. Chill until serving time.

Serves 12

Beatrice White

SCHOOLS DEBATE TOURNAMENT *Since 1990, BJSL has sponsored the annual debate competition presently including the 12 middle schools and 8 senior schools on the island. In 1991, BJSL sent Bermuda's team to the World Schools Debating Championship.*

Christmas Pudding

2¼ cups brown bread crumbs
1½ cups milk
8 ounces suet, chopped
8 ounces dates, chopped
4 ounces mixed candied fruit peel, chopped
8 ounces raisins
8 ounces golden raisins
3 eggs, beaten
½ teaspoon baking soda
½ cup molasses

½ cup brandy or rum
½ teaspoon ground cloves
½ teaspoon mace
½ teaspoon nutmeg
½ teaspoon allspice
2 tablespoons flour
1½ teaspoons baking powder
½ teaspoon vanilla extract
brandy
Hard Sauce or Lemon Sauce (page 207)

Soak the bread crumbs in the milk in a bowl. Add the suet, dates, fruit peel and raisins. Stir in the eggs. Mix the baking soda with the molasses in a cup. Add to the pudding with ½ cup brandy and mix well. Combine the cloves, mace, nutmeg and allspice. Add to the pudding and stir in the flour, baking powder and vanilla.

Pour into 2 large or 3 small pudding dishes. Place in a large pan of boiling water and steam for 2½ hours. Remove from the heat and cool to room temperature. Invert onto serving plates.

Pour additional brandy over the pudding and ignite for a dramatic holiday presentation. Serve with Hard Sauce or Lemon Sauce and garnish with sprigs of holly.

Makes 2 large puddings or 3 small puddings

Cornelia Kempe

Hard Sauce

1/3 cup butter, softened
1 cup sugar or packed brown sugar

3/4 teaspoon vanilla extract or brandy

Cream the butter and sugar in a mixing bowl until light. Add the vanilla and beat until fluffy. Spoon into a covered container and store in the refrigerator for several days before serving. Serve with Christmas Pudding.

Makes about 1 cup

Cornelia Kempe

Lemon Sauce

1/2 cup sugar
1 1/2 tablespoons cornstarch
pinch of salt
1 cup warm water

1 1/2 teaspoons grated lemon zest
2 tablespoons fresh lemon juice
1 tablespoon butter

Mix the sugar, cornstarch and salt in a saucepan. Stir in the water and lemon zest. Cook over low heat for 5 minutes or until clear and thickened, stirring constantly. Remove from the heat and add the lemon juice and butter, stirring until the butter melts. Serve warm or cool with Christmas Pudding.

Makes about 1 1/2 cups

Cornelia Kempe

Bread and Butter Pudding

5 or 6 slices white bread
softened butter
2 ounces dried fruit

2 tablespoons sugar
2 eggs
2 cups cold milk

Spread the bread with butter and cut into triangles. Mix the dried fruit with the sugar in a bowl. Alternate layers of the bread and fruit mixture in a round baking dish. Beat the eggs and add the cold milk; mix well. Pour over the layers and let stand for 1 hour. Bake at 300 degrees for 45 to 60 minutes or until set and light brown.

Serves 4

Annette Cook

Summer Fruit Pudding

8 (¹/₂-inch) slices stale white bread, crusts removed
1¹/₂ pounds mixed soft fruit, such as strawberries, raspberries, currants,
   blueberries and/or black cherries
¹/₂ cup sugar

Line the bottom of a 3-cup soufflé dish or pudding basin with 1 or 2 slices of the bread, covering completely. Line the side with some of the remaining bread, cutting to fit if necessary; the bread should fit closely.

Clean, hull and pit the berries. Combine in a heavy skillet and sprinkle with the sugar. Bring to a simmer over very low heat and cook for 2 to 3 minutes or just until the sugar dissolves and the fruit begins to release juices. Remove and reserve 1 to 2 tablespoons of the juice. Spoon the fruit and remaining juices into the prepared dish.

Cover the fruit with the remaining bread. Place plastic wrap directly on the bread and top with a plate that fits the inside of the dish; weight the plate. Chill in the refrigerator for 8 hours or longer. Remove the weight, plate and plastic wrap. Invert the pudding onto a serving plate and drizzle the reserved juice over any portions of the bread that were not saturated with juice. Serve with whipped cream.

Serves 6

Kathy Suter

Traditional Mincemeat

4 lemons
4 pounds Granny Smith or other tart apples, peeled and finely chopped
2 pounds currants
1 pound seedless raisins
1 pound golden raisins
1 pound mixed candied fruit peel
1½ pounds suet, chopped
4 pounds brown sugar
2 cups sherry
1 cup brandy
1 teaspoon cinnamon
1 teaspoon mace
½ teaspoon nutmeg
½ teaspoon cloves
½ teaspoon allspice
½ teaspoon salt

Cut the lemons into quarters and discard the seeds. Chop the unpeeled lemons in a food processor. Combine with the apples, currants, raisins, candied fruit peel and suet in a large bowl. Add the brown sugar, sherry, brandy, cinnamon, mace, nutmeg, cloves, allspice and salt and mix well. Spoon into a sterilised 1-gallon container and seal.

Bermudians substitute black rum for the sherry and brandy in this recipe. They use it for Christmas mincemeat tarts, to serve over vanilla ice cream or to combine with apples in pies.

Makes 1 gallon   *Cornelia Kempe*

KING EDWARD VII MEMORIAL HOSPITAL
RAPE CRISIS ROOM *In 1999, BJSL spent $12,000 furnishing this important facility.*

Simple Ice Cream Dessert

12 scoops chocolate ice cream
6 waffle cookie ice cream cups
6 ounces Kahlúa
12 tablespoons toasted coconut

Place 2 scoops of the ice cream in each cookie cup. Place on serving plates. Drizzle with the Kahlúa and sprinkle with the coconut. Serve immediately.

Serves 6   *Pam Kempe*

Syllabub

1 cup minus 2 tablespoons sugar
juice and finely grated zest of
   3 large lemons
11 ounces vermouth or other
   white wine
3 ounces brandy
4 cups whipping cream
lemon slices

Combine the sugar, lemon juice, lemon zest, wine and brandy in a double boiler. Cook over simmering water until the sugar dissolves, stirring constantly. Cool to room temperature.

Whip the cream in a mixing bowl until soft peaks form. Fold into the cooled mixture. Spoon into Champagne glasses and chill for 2 hours or up to 6 hours; the mixture will separate slightly in the bottom of the glasses. Garnish with lemon slices and additional grated lemon zest to serve.

Serves 12   *Susan Titterton*

Carrot Cake

with Cream Cheese Frosting

CAKE

2 cups sugar
3/4 cup canola oil
4 eggs
1 teaspoon vanilla extract
2 cups flour
2 teaspoons baking powder
1 1/2 teaspoons baking soda
2 teaspoons cinnamon
2 cups shredded carrots
1 (8-ounce) can crushed pineapple, drained

CREAM CHEESE FROSTING

6 ounces cream cheese, softened
6 tablespoons (3/4 stick) margarine, softened
2 cups icing sugar
1 teaspoon vanilla extract

For the cake, combine the sugar and canola oil in a medium mixing bowl and mix well. Beat in the eggs 1 at a time. Stir in the vanilla. Add the flour, baking powder, baking soda and cinnamon and mix well. Add the carrots and pineapple and stir just until moistened.

Spoon into a greased 9×13-inch baking pan. Bake at 350 degrees for 45 minutes or until a wooden pick comes out clean and the cake begins to pull from the sides of the pan. Cool on a wire rack.

For the frosting, combine the cream cheese, margarine, icing sugar and vanilla in a bowl and mix until smooth. Spread over the cooled cake.

You can bake the cake in a bundt pan for 55 minutes if preferred. Cool in the pan for 15 minutes and then remove to a wire rack to cool completely. Frost as above.

You may find any cake easier to frost if it is chilled in the refrigerator prior to spreading with the room-temperature frosting.

Serves 12 to 16

Christine Caton

Inside-Out Chocolate Cake

1 (2-layer) package devil's food cake mix
1 (3^1/$_2$-ounce) package chocolate instant pudding mix
1^3/$_4$ cups milk
2 eggs
12 ounces (2 cups) semisweet chocolate chips
icing sugar

Combine the cake mix, pudding mix, milk and eggs in a bowl and mix well by hand. Stir in the chocolate chips. Spoon into a greased and floured bundt pan or tube pan.

Bake at 350 degrees for 1 to 1^1/$_2$ hours or until the cake tests done. Cool in the pan for 10 minutes and invert onto a wire rack to cool completely. Place on a serving plate and sprinkle with icing sugar.

You can also coat a greased cake pan with sugar rather than flour. It makes for a sweeter taste and does not leave a flour film on the cake.

Serves 24   *Sally Gibbons*

Bacardi® Gold Rum and Nut Cake

CAKE

1 cup chopped pecans or walnuts
1 (2-layer) package yellow cake mix
1 (13-ounce) package vanilla instant pudding mix
1/2 cup Bacardi® Gold Rum
4 eggs
1/2 cup vegetable oil
1/2 cup water

BACARDI® GOLD RUM GLAZE

1/4 cup (1/2 stick) butter
1 cup sugar
1/4 cup water
1/2 cup Bacardi® Gold Rum

For the cake, sprinkle the pecans in a greased and floured 12-cup bundt pan. Combine the cake mix, pudding mix, rum, eggs, oil and water in a mixing bowl and beat at low speed until moistened. Beat at high speed for 2 minutes.

Spoon into the prepared bundt pan. Bake at 325 degrees for 1 hour or until a tester comes out clean. Cool in the pan for 15 minutes and invert onto a serving plate.

For the glaze, melt the butter in a saucepan. Stir in the sugar, water and rum. Bring to a boil and boil for 5 minutes, stirring constantly. Remove from the heat. Prick the cake with a fork. Spoon and brush evenly over the cake.

Serves 12

KING EDWARD VII MEMORIAL HOSPITAL CHRISTMAS BAG PROJECT *For 50 years, BJSL has provided gift packages containing items donated by local merchants to those who must spend Christmas in the hospital.*

Bride's Wedding Cake

8 pounds dark raisins
2 pounds dates, chopped
2 pounds mixed candied fruit, chopped
1 pound red candied cherries, cut into halves
1 pound green candied cherries, cut into halves
8 candied pineapple slices, cut into small pieces
4 cups black rum
9 cups flour
4 teaspoons baking soda
4 teaspoons cinnamon

4 teaspoons allspice
4 teaspoons nutmeg
1 tablespoon mace
1 teaspoon ground cloves
4 teaspoons salt
2 pounds (8 sticks) butter, softened
2 pounds brown sugar
24 eggs
1 cup molasses
Royal Icing (page 215)

Combine the raisins, dates, mixed fruit, cherries, pineapple and rum in a large bowl. Marinate in the refrigerator for 1 week or longer, stirring occasionally.

Combine the fruit mixture with 2 cups of the flour in a bowl and toss to coat well. Mix the remaining flour with the baking soda, cinnamon, allspice, nutmeg, mace, cloves and salt.

Cream the butter and brown sugar in a large mixing bowl until light and fluffy. Beat in the eggs 1 at a time. Add the molasses and mix well. Beat in the flour mixture gradually. Fold in the fruit mixture with a wooden spoon; the batter will be moist.

Line one 11- or 12-inch, one 9- or 10-inch and one 6- or 8-inch round or square pan with brown paper. Spoon the batter into the cake pans. Place in a 300-degree oven and bake the largest layer for 2 1/2 to 3 hours or until a wooden pick inserted in the center comes out clean; remove the smaller layers as they test done by the same method. Cool in the pans for 10 minutes and remove to a wire rack to cool completely.

Spread Royal Icing between the layers and over the top and sides of the layers. Let the cake stand for 24 hours before decorating to allow the icing to set. You may cover the cake layers with a thin layer of marzipan before spreading with the icing if preferred. You may also cover the entire cake with thin sheets of silver leaf and decorate as desired.

The cake can be stored in large airtight tins lined with waxed paper for several weeks or wrapped in plastic wrap and frozen for several months. Thaw the cake at least a week before icing. Reduce the recipe by 1/2 to produce only the largest cake layer, or by 1/4 to produce only the 2 largest layers.

Makes 100 small pieces

Cornelia Kempe

Royal Icing

4 egg whites
2 pounds icing sugar

Combine the egg whites with ¼ cup of the icing sugar in a large mixing bowl. Beat for 3 minutes. Add the remaining icing sugar gradually, beating constantly until the sugar is completely incorporated and stiff peaks form.

Spread immediately between the layers and over the top and sides of the cake with a straight-blade spatula to create a smooth, flat finish; the icing will begin to set right away and should be spread immediately. Let stand for 24 hours or longer before decorating.

Ices 1 cake

Carolyn Toogood

TRADITIONAL BRIDE'S CAKE

The traditional Bermudian bride's cake is a fruitcake, symbolic of a fruitful marriage. It is baked in two or three layers, which are then covered with marzipan, stacked, and spread with Royal Icing. The cake is then covered with sheets of real silver leaf and decorated with Bermuda roses and ivy. It is also traditional to keep the top layer of the bride's cake and freeze it until the christening of the couple's first child.

MARZIPAN

This gently textured sweet is made of almond paste, sugar, and, often, egg whites. It is used as a filling for sweet breads and cakes as well as candies.

Groom's Plain Pound Cake

1 pound butter, softened
1 pound (2 cups) sugar
12 egg yolks
12 egg whites, stiffly beaten
1 pound (4 cups) flour
1/2 teaspoon baking powder
2 1/2 teaspoons vanilla extract
3/4 teaspoon lemon essence
1 1/2 cups rum

Cream the butter and sugar in a mixing bowl until light and fluffy. Beat in the egg yolks 1 at a time. Add the egg whites gradually, mixing well after each addition. Add the flour, baking powder, vanilla, lemon essence and rum in the order listed, mixing well after each addition.

Line a 12-inch cake pan with waxed paper; grease and flour the waxed paper. Spoon the batter into the prepared pan. Bake at 225 degrees for 2 1/2 to 3 hours or until a wooden pick comes out clean. Cool in the pan for 10 minutes and remove to a wire rack. Remove the waxed paper and cool the cake completely.

You may frost the cake with Royal Icing (page 215) and/or cover with gold leaf if desired. Cut into 1-inch slices to serve.

Serves 30   *Carolyn Toogood*

Traditional Fruitcake

3 cups seedless raisins
3 cups golden raisins
1/2 cup candied cherries
1 cup chopped mixed candied fruit peel
1/2 cup dark rum or brandy
1 cup walnuts, chopped (optional)
1 3/4 cups flour
1/4 teaspoon baking soda

1 teaspoon cinnamon
1 teaspoon allspice
1/4 teaspoon nutmeg
1/2 teaspoon salt
1 cup shortening
1 cup packed brown sugar
6 eggs
1/2 cup molasses

Combine the raisins, cherries and fruit peel with the rum in a bowl and mix well. Marinate in the refrigerator for 1 week, stirring occasionally.

Add the walnuts and 1/4 cup of the flour to the fruit mixture and toss to coat well. Combine the remaining flour with the baking soda, cinnamon, allspice, nutmeg and salt in a bowl.

Cream the shortening and brown sugar in a mixing bowl until light and fluffy. Beat in the eggs 1 at a time. Beat in the molasses. Add the flour mixture and mix well. Fold in the fruit and walnut mixture.

Spoon into two 9-inch cake pans lined with heavy waxed paper, filling about 2/3 full. Bake at 300 degrees for 2 hours or until a wooden pick inserted into the center comes out clean. Cool in the pans for 10 minutes and remove to a wire rack to cool completely. Store in airtight containers for up to 1 month. Sprinkle with icing sugar to serve.

You may also bake the batter in 2 waxed paper-lined 5x9-inch loaf pans or an angel food cake pan. Tossing the raisins or other fruit with the flour will keep them evenly distributed in the cake.

Makes 2 cakes

Cornelia Kempe

Lovable Lemon Cake

1 (3-ounce) package lemon gelatin
$^3/_4$ cup boiling water
4 eggs, beaten
1 (2-layer) package lemon cake mix

$^3/_4$ cup vegetable oil
juice of 2 lemons
2 cups icing sugar

Dissolve the gelatin in the boiling water in a bowl; let stand until cool. Beat in the eggs. Add the cake mix and oil and mix well. Spoon into a 9×13-inch cake pan. Bake at 350 degrees until the cake tests done.

Mix the lemon juice and icing sugar in a bowl until smooth. Pierce holes all the way through the warm cake at 2-inch intervals. Drizzle with the sugar mixture. Let stand until cool.

You may cut the cake into individual servings with a round cutter if desired.

Serves 8

Carolyn Toogood

Perfect Apple Pie

1 recipe Shortcrust Pastry (below)
3/4 cup sugar
1 tablespoon flour
1/2 teaspoon cinnamon
1/4 teaspoon nutmeg

1/8 teaspoon salt
5 cups thickly sliced peeled Granny Smith apples
1 tablespoon lemon juice
2 tablespoons butter or margarine

Roll half the pastry on a floured surface and fit into a 9-inch pie plate. Mix the sugar, flour, cinnamon, nutmeg and salt in a bowl. Add the apples and toss to coat evenly. Spread in the prepared pie plate. Sprinkle with the lemon juice and dot with the butter.

Roll the remaining pastry and place over the apples. Trim and flute the edge of the pastry. Bake at 425 degrees for 40 to 45 minutes or until the apples are tender and the pastry is golden brown.

Serves 6 to 8

Beatrice White

Shortcrust Pastry

2 cups flour
1/2 teaspoon salt
1/4 cup (1/2 stick) margarine, softened

1/4 cup shortening
4 to 6 tablespoons ice water

Sift the flour and salt into a bowl. Cut in the margarine and shortening with a round-blade knife; rub with the fingertips to incorporate completely. Add 4 tablespoons water gradually and mix until the mixture begins to come together; add additional water if necessary. Shape into 2 smooth balls. Use as directed in a pie recipe.

Reduce the recipe by half for a single-crust pie. Fit the rolled dough into the pie plate and fill. Bake the filled pie at 400 to 425 degrees for 15 to 20 minutes. Reduce the oven temperature to 350 degrees for the remainder of the cooking time.

Makes 2 pastries

Carolyn Toogood

BAKING WITH BANANAS

While the taste and texture of most vegetables does not continue to improve after they are harvested, the qualities of many fruits are enhanced by aging awhile after being picked. This is especially true of bananas and avocados, both grown in Bermuda. Overripe and mushy or even "black" bananas are at their peak of sweetness and produce the tastiest breads, muffins, desserts, and sauces. You can freeze extra bananas in their perfectly ripe state to be used for future baking needs.

Banoffee Pie

1 (7-ounce) package chocolate digestive cookies, crushed
$^1/_4$ cup ($^1/_2$ stick) butter, melted
9 ounces sweetened condensed milk
3 bananas, sliced
1 cup grated chocolate
1 cup whipping cream
shaved chocolate

Mix the cookie crumbs and butter in a bowl. Spoon into a 9-inch pie plate and press over the bottom and side to form a crust. Bake at 350 degrees for 5 minutes. Cool to room temperature.

Place the sweetened condensed milk in a 2-quart microwave-safe bowl. Microwave on Medium for 4 minutes, stirring every 2 minutes. Microwave on Medium-Low for 20 to 26 minutes or until caramelised, stirring every 4 minutes for the first 16 minutes and every 2 minutes for the remaining minutes. Spread over the cooled crust.

Arrange the sliced bananas over the pie and sprinkle with the grated chocolate. Whip the cream in a mixing bowl until soft peaks form. Spread over the pie and sprinkle with shaved chocolate. Chill for 2 hours or longer.

Serves 8

Audrey Smith

Blueberry Pie

3/4 cup sugar
3 tablespoons cornstarch
1/8 teaspoon salt
1/4 cup water

4 cups fresh blueberries
1 tablespoon butter
1 tablespoon lemon juice
1 baked (9- or 10-inch) pie shell

Mix the sugar, cornstarch and salt in a saucepan. Blend in the water and add 2 cups of the blueberries. Bring to a boil over medium heat and cook until thickened and clear, stirring constantly. Remove from the heat and stir in the butter and lemon juice. Cool to room temperature.

Spread the remaining 2 cups blueberries in the pie shell and top with the cooled blueberry mixture. Chill until serving time. Serve with whipped cream.

Serves 8

Paula Dilney-Friend

**JUICING
CITRUS FRUIT**

*To obtain the most juice
from citrus fruit,
microwave it for 10 to
15 seconds. Then roll it on
a work surface, pressing
gently. The heat and
pressure help to release
the juice from the fruit.*

Lemon Pie

1 unbaked pie shell
1 cup castor (superfine) sugar
1 cup cream
4 eggs
1 cup lemon juice

Bake the pie shell at 350 degrees for 20 minutes or until it begins to brown. Remove from the oven and reduce the oven temperature to 315 degrees.

Combine the sugar, cream, eggs and lemon juice in a food processor and process until smooth. Spoon into the partially baked pie shell. Bake for 20 minutes longer or until the filling is set.

Chill until serving time. Serve with whipped cream. You may substitute lime juice for the lemon juice to prepare lime pie.

Serves 6   *Tegan Smith*

Lemon Chiffon Pie

1½ teaspoons unflavoured gelatin
⅓ cup cold water
4 egg yolks
juice and grated zest of 1 lemon
½ cup sugar
4 egg whites
½ cup sugar
pinch of salt (optional)
1 baked pie shell
whipped cream

Dissolve the gelatin in the cold water in a small bowl. Combine the egg yolks, lemon juice, lemon zest and ½ cup sugar in a double boiler and mix well. Cook over simmering water until thickened, stirring constantly. Add the gelatin and stir to dissolve completely. Cool to room temperature.

Beat the egg whites in a mixing bowl until frothy. Add ½ cup sugar and a pinch of salt gradually, beating constantly until stiff peaks form. Fold gently into the cooled egg yolk mixture. Spoon into the pie shell. Spread with whipped cream at serving time.

Serves 8

Mrs. C. Vail Zuill, MBE
Janette R. Zuill, Founding President

FOUNDING THE BJSL *Following the Junior League of America, the Bermuda Junior Service League (BJSL) was founded in 1936 by Mrs. C. Vail Zuill. During the early years, the League grew in a variety of activities that stemmed from its original concept of helping the King Edward VII Memorial Hospital (KEMH), the Welfare Society, and the Lady Cubbitt Compassion Association (LCCA). In 1953, the BJSL was approached to assist the KEMH with the formation of a Hospital Auxiliary. As a result, our Life Members formed the Women's Hospital Auxiliary (Pink Ladies), which today is an indispensable separate organization.*

The variety of loquat grown in Bermuda is the yellow-orange plum-like fruit that ripens in the late winter or early spring. The crisp and juicy flesh is pale yellow and has a delicate tangy flavour. Loquats were imported originally to persuade local birds to stop eating expensive citrus. Bermudians eat loquats straight off the tree, stewed or cooked in chutneys, pies or jams; the juice is served in drinks.

Loquat Pie

2 apples
9 cups seeded loquats
3 cups sugar, or to taste
2 tablespoons cornstarch
cinnamon, ginger and salt to taste
1 unbaked pie shell

Peel and slice the apples, discarding the cores and seeds. Combine the loquats and apples in a saucepan and cook over low heat until the fruit is tender and the juices are released. Stir in the sugar, cornstarch, cinnamon, ginger and salt. Cook until thickened, stirring constantly.

Spoon into the pie shell and bake at 425 degrees for 15 to 20 minutes. Cover the edge of the pie with foil and bake for 25 to 30 minutes longer or until the crust is golden brown. Serve warm with vanilla ice cream.

Serves 8

Dawn Dunstan

Tropical Pie

1 (11-ounce) can mandarin oranges, drained
1 (11-ounce) can crushed pineapple, drained
1 (14-ounce) can sweetened condensed milk
6 tablespoons lemon juice
16 ounces whipped topping
2 (9- or 10-inch) graham cracker pie shells

Combine the oranges and pineapple in a bowl and mix well. Stir the sweetened condensed milk and lemon juice together in a bowl. Add the fruit and whipped topping and mix gently. Spoon into the pie shells. Chill for 2 hours or longer. Garnish with additional fruit.

Makes 2 pies

Paula Dilney-Friend

CRISP CRUSTS

For berry, fruit, or custard pies, beat egg whites with 2 teaspoons water and brush over the crust before adding the filling. This will prevent the crust from getting soggy.

Pear Pie

3 fresh pears
1 unbaked (9- or 10-inch) pie shell
1 cup sugar
$^1/_4$ cup flour
$^1/_4$ cup ($^1/_2$ stick) butter, melted
2 eggs
1 teaspoon vanilla extract

Cut the pears into halves lengthwise and discard the cores. Arrange cut side down in the pie shell. Combine the sugar, flour, butter, eggs and vanilla in a bowl and beat until smooth. Pour over the pears. Bake at 325 degrees for 40 to 45 minutes or until the custard is firm.

Serves 8

Paula Dilney-Friend

KING EDWARD VII MEMORIAL HOSPITAL LIBRARY *BJSL members donated magazine subscriptions, circulated a library cart to patients, and replenished the reading materials in various waiting and reception areas.*

Pumpkin Spice Pie

2 tablespoons sugar
1 tablespoon flour
1/8 teaspoon cinnamon or ginger
1 unbaked (9-inch) pie shell
2 cups mashed cooked pumpkin
2/3 cup packed brown sugar
2 teaspoons cinnamon
1 teaspoon ginger

1/2 teaspoon ground cloves
1/2 teaspoon nutmeg
1/2 teaspoon allspice
1/2 teaspoon salt
2 eggs
1 (14-ounce) can sweetened condensed milk
2 teaspoons dark rum (optional)
1 egg

Mix the sugar, flour and 1/8 teaspoon cinnamon in a small bowl. Sprinkle over the bottom and side of the pie shell. Combine the pumpkin, brown sugar, 2 teaspoons cinnamon, ginger, cloves, nutmeg, allspice and salt in a large bowl and mix well. Beat 2 eggs with the sweetened condensed milk and rum in a bowl. Add to the pumpkin mixture and stir to mix well.

Pour the pumpkin filling into the prepared pie shell. Beat the remaining egg and brush over the crust with a pastry brush. Bake at 425 degrees for 15 minutes. Reduce the oven temperature to 350 degrees and bake for 35 to 40 minutes longer or until a knife inserted into the center comes out clean.

Cool completely on a wire rack. Store in the refrigerator until time to serve. You may top the baked pie with Pumpkin Pie Topping (below) if desired and bake or broil just until the topping melts.

Serves 8

Elizabeth Zalinger

Pumpkin Pie Topping

1 cup chopped walnuts or pecans
1 cup packed brown sugar

1/4 cup (1/2 stick) butter or margarine, softened

Combine the walnuts, brown sugar and butter in a bowl and mix until crumbly. Sprinkle over hot pumpkin pie. Bake at 425 degrees just until the topping begins to melt. You may also broil until melted, watching carefully to prevent burning.

Tops 1 pie

Cornelia Kempe

Homemade Brownies

4 ounces unsweetened chocolate
²/₃ cup shortening
2 cups sugar
4 eggs
1 teaspoon vanilla extract
1¼ cups flour
1 teaspoon baking powder
1 teaspoon salt
1 cup chopped nuts (optional)

Melt the chocolate with the shortening in a saucepan over low heat. Stir to blend and remove from the heat. Add the sugar, eggs and vanilla and mix well. Stir in the flour, baking powder, salt and nuts.

Spread evenly in a greased 9×13-inch baking pan. Bake at 350 degrees for 30 minutes. Cool on a wire rack and cut into squares.

Makes 2 dozen

Ardleigh Young

Cream Cheese Brownies

5 tablespoons butter, softened
6 ounces cream cheese, softened
1/3 cup sugar
2 eggs
2 tablespoons flour
3/4 teaspoon vanilla extract
1 large package brownie mix
3 eggs
2 tablespoons water

Cream the butter and cream cheese in a mixing bowl until smooth. Beat in the sugar, 2 eggs, flour and vanilla.

Prepare the brownie mix using 3 eggs and 2 tablespoons water. Spread half the brownie mixture in a greased 9×13-inch baking pan. Spread the cream cheese mixture in the prepared pan and spread the remaining brownie mixture over the cream cheese layer. Cut through the layers with a knife to swirl.

Bake at 350 degrees for 35 to 40 minutes or until the brownies test done. Cool on a wire rack. Cut into squares. Use a plastic knife to cut warm brownies to avoid messy clumps.

Makes 2 dozen

Kelly Marshall

COMMUNITY SERVICE TAG DAYS *BJSL volunteers help raise money for such charities as The Women's Resource Centre, The Haven, SPCA, The Salvation Army, LCCA, Bermuda Autism Support & Education Society, The Family Centre, The Committee of 25 for Handicapped Children, and the Bermuda TB, Cancer & Health Association.*

Chocolate Mint Brownies

1 cup (2 sticks) butter
4 ounces unsweetened chocolate
2 cups sugar
4 eggs
1 cup flour
1/2 teaspoon salt
1 teaspoon vanilla extract

1/2 cup (1 stick) butter, melted
2 cups icing sugar
1 tablespoon peppermint extract
1 or 2 drops of green food coloring
6 tablespoons (3/4 stick) butter
8 ounces chocolate chips

Melt 1 cup butter with the unsweetened chocolate in a double boiler, stirring to blend well; remove from the heat. Combine the sugar, eggs, flour, salt and vanilla in a bowl and mix well. Stir in the chocolate mixture. Spread in a greased 9×13-inch baking pan. Bake at 350 degrees for 25 minutes. Cool on a wire rack.

Combine 1/2 cup butter, the icing sugar, peppermint extract and food coloring in a mixing bowl and mix until smooth. Spread over the cooked brownie layer.

Melt 6 tablespoons butter with the chocolate chips in a double boiler, stirring to blend well. Spread immediately over the mint layer, tilting the pan to spread evenly. Chill in the refrigerator for several hours. Cut into small squares. Store in the refrigerator or freezer.

Makes 5 dozen

Beth Lindgren

Magic Cookie Bars

1/2 cup (1 stick) margarine, melted
1 1/2 cups graham cracker crumbs
3 tablespoons sugar
1 cup coarsely chopped walnuts

6 ounces (1 cup) chocolate chips and/or
  butterscotch chips
1 (3 1/2-ounce) package or can flaked coconut
1 (14-ounce) can sweetened condensed milk

Spread the margarine in a 9×13-inch baking pan. Add the graham cracker crumbs and sugar and mix well. Press evenly over the bottom of the pan. Sprinkle with the walnuts, chocolate chips and coconut. Drizzle with the sweetened condensed milk.

Bake at 325 to 350 degrees for 25 minutes or until a wooden pick inserted into the center comes out clean. Cool on a wire rack. Cut into squares.

Makes 2 dozen

Kim Paterson

Sin City Bars

1 (2-layer) package German's chocolate cake mix
3/4 cup (1 1/2 sticks) butter, melted
1/3 cup milk
1 (14-ounce) package caramel candies, unwrapped

1/3 cup milk
12 ounces (2 cups) chocolate chips
1 cup chopped pecans to taste (optional)

Combine the cake mix, melted butter and 1/3 cup milk in a bowl and mix well. Press half the mixture evenly over the bottom of a 9×13-inch baking pan. Bake at 325 degrees for 10 minutes.

Melt the caramels with 1/3 cup milk in a saucepan over low heat, stirring to blend well. Pour over the partially baked layer and spread evenly. Sprinkle with the chocolate chips and pecans. Work the remaining chocolate mixture into thin layers with the fingers and layer over the top.

Bake for 15 to 19 minutes longer or until the chocolate layers test done. Cool on a wire rack for 10 minutes. Garnish with additional chocolate and walnuts if desired. Cut into bars or squares.

Makes 2 dozen

Wendi Ryland

Peanut Butter Squares

1¹/₃ cups icing sugar
¹/₄ cup packed dark brown sugar
³/₄ cup creamy peanut butter
¹/₄ cup (¹/₂ stick) unsalted butter

8 ounces milk chocolate
4 ounces semisweet chocolate
1 tablespoon butter

Combine the icing sugar, brown sugar, peanut butter and ¹/₄ cup butter in a mixing bowl and mix until smooth. Press into a 9×13-inch dish lined with waxed paper.

Combine the milk chocolate, semisweet chocolate and 1 tablespoon butter in a microwave-safe bowl. Microwave on Medium until melted; stir to blend well. Spread over the peanut butter mixture. Chill in the refrigerator until set. Cut into squares.

Makes 2 dozen

Mary Mello

Eatmore Bars

12 ounces (2 cups) chocolate chips
1 cup corn syrup
¹/₄ cup creamy peanut butter
2 cups crisp rice cereal
2 cups salted peanuts

Combine the chocolate chips, corn syrup and peanut butter in a microwave-safe bowl. Microwave on Medium until the chocolate chips and peanut butter melt; stir to mix well. Stir in the cereal and peanuts.

Spread evenly in a greased 9×13-inch dish. Chill in the refrigerator. Cut into bars to serve.

Makes 2 dozen

Paula Dilney-Friend

Date Dainties

1¹/4 cups flour
1¹/4 cups rolled oats
¹/2 cup packed brown sugar
1 teaspoon baking powder
¹/2 teaspoon salt

³/4 cup (1¹/2 sticks) butter
1 cup chopped dates
¹/2 cup boiling water
2 tablespoons cooking sherry
¹/2 cup packed brown sugar

Mix the flour, oats, ¹/2 cup brown sugar, baking powder and salt in a bowl. Cut in the butter until crumbly. Spread half the mixture in a greased and floured 9×13-inch baking pan. Combine the dates, water, sherry and ¹/2 cup brown sugar in a bowl and mix well. Spread in the prepared baking pan. Crumble the remaining oats mixture over the top and press down gently.

Bake at 375 degrees for 20 minutes. Cut into squares immediately and remove to a wire rack to cool completely.

You can soften brown sugar that has become hard by placing a slice of soft bread in the package and closing the bag tightly. The sugar will be soft again in a few hours.

Makes 2 dozen

Mrs. C. Vail Zuill, MBE
Janette R. Zuill, Founding President

Russian Tea Cookies

1 cup (2 sticks) butter, softened
¹/2 cup sugar
1 teaspoon vanilla extract
2¹/4 cups sifted flour

¹/4 teaspoon salt
³/4 cup finely chopped walnuts
icing sugar

Cream the butter, sugar and vanilla in a mixing bowl until light and fluffy. Mix the flour, salt and walnuts in a bowl. Add to the creamed mixture and mix to form a dough. Wrap in plastic wrap and chill in the refrigerator. Shape into 1-inch balls and arrange on an ungreased cookie sheet. Bake at 400 degrees for 10 to 12 minutes or until golden brown. Roll immediately in icing sugar and cool on a wire rack. Roll again in icing sugar. Store in an airtight container for several weeks.

You can easily double this recipe.

Makes 3 to 4 dozen

Cornelia Kempe

Cranberry Cookies

3 cups flour
1 teaspoon baking powder
$1/4$ teaspoon baking soda
$1/2$ teaspoon salt
$1/4$ cup ground walnuts
$2/3$ cup (1 stick plus 2 tablespoons) butter, softened
1 cup sugar

1 cup packed brown sugar
1 egg
2 tablespoons lemon juice
$2^1/2$ cups fresh cranberries, cut into halves
1 cup chopped walnuts

Mix the flour, baking powder, baking soda, salt and ground walnuts in a bowl. Combine the butter, sugar, brown sugar, egg and lemon juice in a bowl and beat until smooth. Add the flour mixture and mix well. Stir in the cranberries and chopped walnuts.

Drop by heaping teaspoonfuls 2 inches apart onto a cookie sheet. Bake at 350 degrees for 16 to 18 minutes or until golden brown; do not underbake. Cool on the cookie sheet for 5 minutes and remove to a wire rack to cool completely. Store in an airtight container.

You can place a slice of bread in a container of freshly baked cookies to keep them softer and chewier.

Makes 4 dozen

Christa Cooper

Nutmeg Cookies

3/4 cup (1 1/2 sticks) margarine, softened
1 cup sugar
1 egg
1/2 teaspoon salt
1 teaspoon vanilla extract
2 teaspoons nutmeg
2 cups flour
1/2 teaspoon baking soda

Cream the margarine and sugar in a mixing bowl until light and fluffy. Beat in the egg, salt, vanilla and nutmeg. Add the flour and baking soda and mix well.

Drop onto greased cookie sheets and press with a wet fork to flatten. Bake at 350 degrees for 10 to 12 minutes or until golden brown. Cool on the cookie sheets for 5 minutes and remove to a wire rack to cool completely. Store in an airtight container.

Makes 3 dozen   *Sally Gibbons*

STUFF THE BUS *Starting in Fall 2003, BJSL provided school supplies for all children entering the public school system in Primary One.*

Millionaire's Shortbread

6 tablespoons (³/₄ stick) butter, softened
¹/₄ cup sugar
1¹/₄ cups flour
¹/₂ cup packed brown sugar
2 tablespoons corn syrup

¹/₂ (14-ounce) can sweetened condensed milk
¹/₂ cup (1 stick) butter
3 ounces bittersweet chocolate
1 tablespoon butter

Cream 6 tablespoons butter and the sugar in a mixing bowl until light and fluffy. Add the flour gradually, mixing to form a dough. Press into a greased 8×8-inch baking pan. Bake at 375 degrees for 20 to 25 minutes or until golden brown. Cool completely on a wire rack.

Combine the brown sugar, corn syrup, sweetened condensed milk and ¹/₂ cup butter in a saucepan. Bring to a boil and reduce the heat. Simmer for 5 minutes, stirring constantly. Beat with a wooden spoon until fluffy and pour over the cooled layer. Chill in the refrigerator.

Melt the chocolate with 1 tablespoon butter in a saucepan over low heat, stirring to blend well. Pour over the layers and let stand until cool. Cut into small squares or bars.

Makes 2 dozen

Susan Smith

Spice Cookies

HOLIDAY COOKIE ORNAMENTS

Use cookie cutters in holiday shapes, such as stars, trees, candy canes, hearts, bunnies, or pumpkins. Pierce a hole in the tops of the cookies with a straw before baking. Cool the cookies, string with ribbons, and hang.

2 teaspoons baking soda
2 tablespoons water or milk
3 1/4 cups flour
2 teaspoons cinnamon
1 1/2 teaspoons ginger
1 1/2 teaspoons ground cloves
1 cup (2 sticks) butter, softened
1 1/2 cups sugar
1 egg
1 tablespoon dark corn syrup
2 tablespoons molasses

Dissolve the baking soda in the water in a cup. Sift the flour with the cinnamon, ginger and cloves. Cream the butter and sugar in a mixing bowl until light and fluffy. Beat in the egg, corn syrup and molasses. Add the baking soda solution. Fold in the flour mixture. Shape into a ball and wrap in plastic wrap. Chill for 2 hours or longer.

Roll the dough thin on a lightly floured surface. Cut out as desired and place on an ungreased cookie sheet. Bake at 350 degrees for 8 to 10 minutes or just until the edges begin to brown. Cool on the cookie sheet for 5 minutes and remove to a wire rack to cool completely.

You can roll cookie dough between 2 sheets of parchment paper to make the dough easier to handle, and cleanup is a breeze.

Makes 4 dozen

Erin Anderson

Yo-Yo Cookies

2 cups (4 sticks) butter, softened
$^1/_4$ cup icing sugar
1 teaspoon vanilla extract
$^3/_4$ cup flour
$^1/_4$ cup custard powder
1 can prepared vanilla icing

Cream the butter, icing sugar and vanilla in a mixing bowl until light and fluffy. Add the flour and custard powder and mix well. Shape into small balls and place on a parchment-lined cookie sheet. Press with a fork to flatten.

Bake at 350 degrees for 20 minutes. Cool on the cookie sheet for 5 minutes and remove to a wire rack to cool completely.

Spread half the cookies with the icing and top with the remaining cookies to resemble yo-yos.

Makes 1 dozen double cookies

Paula Dilney-Friend

A PLAYGROUND AT WINDREACH RECREATIONAL VILLAGE *BJSL donated the playground equipment, raised money for a ramp to be built and for the construction of a tebin (a cross between a tent and a cabin), and donated funds to Riding for the Disabled.*

Loquat Sauce for Ice Cream

1 quart water
8 ounces loquats
1/4 cup lemon juice
2 cups loquat juice
2 cups sugar

Bring the water to a boil in a saucepan. Reduce the heat to low and add the loquats and lemon juice. Cook for 5 minutes or just until the skins loosen. Drain, reserving the liquid. Cool the loquats and discard the skins and seeds. Combine the loquat juice with the sugar in a saucepan. Cook for 20 minutes or to 230 to 234 degrees on a candy thermometer. Let stand until cool. Add the loquats and mix gently. Chill until serving time. Serve over ice cream.

Makes 3 cups

Deborah Titterton Narraway

Best-Ever Fudge Sauce

3 ounces unsweetened chocolate
1/4 cup (1/2 stick) butter
1 cup icing sugar
1/2 cup heavy cream
1 teaspoon vanilla extract
2 tablespoons favourite liqueur (optional)

Melt the chocolate with the butter in a saucepan, stirring to blend well. Add the icing sugar and beat until smooth. Heat over low heat if necessary to dissolve any lumps, beating constantly until smooth; remove from the heat. Stir in the cream gradually. Add the vanilla and liqueur and mix well. Serve warm over ice cream; serve the ice cream in meringue cups is desired.

You may store unused sauce in the refrigerator and reheat to serve. The recipe can be doubled easily.

Serves 6

Jane Spurling

Espresso Chocolate Fudge

2 tablespoons instant espresso powder
$^1/_2$ cup water
1$^1/_2$ cups sugar
$^3/_4$ cup sweetened condensed milk
$^1/_3$ cup heavy cream
$^1/_4$ cup ($^1/_2$ stick) unsalted butter
6 ounces bittersweet or semisweet chocolate, chopped
1 ounce unsweetened chocolate, chopped
$^1/_4$ cup marshmallow creme
1 teaspoon vanilla extract

Line an 8x8-inch dish with foil, allowing the foil to overlap the edges. Dissolve the espresso powder in the water in a large saucepan. Add the sugar, sweetened condensed milk, cream and butter. Cook over medium heat until the sugar dissolves, stirring constantly. Increase the heat to high and bring to a boil. Reduce the heat to medium and cook for 12 minutes, stirring gently.

Combine the bittersweet chocolate, unsweetened chocolate, marshmallow creme and vanilla in a bowl. Add the hot espresso mixture immediately and stir for 3 minutes or until the chocolates melt and the mixture thickens slightly. Spoon into the prepared dish and smooth the top with a rubber spatula.

Chill in the refrigerator for 2 hours or until firm enough to cut. Lift from the dish using the foil overlap; cut into squares.

Makes 30 pieces

Carolyn Toogood

SHELLY BAY PLAYGROUND & PARK *The park has been adopted by BJSL. The playground was fully funded by the League, and members clean up the park four times a year.*

Marbled Chocolate Almond Bark

6 ounces (1 cup) semisweet chocolate chips
1 cup whole unsalted almonds
12 ounces (2 cups) white chocolate chips
1 cup whole unsalted almonds

Sprinkle the chocolate chips in a single layer in a microwave-safe dish. Microwave on High for 1 minute and 40 seconds or until shiny. Stir until smooth with a rubber spatula and stir in 1 cup almonds.

Sprinkle the white chocolate chips in a single layer in a microwave-safe dish. Microwave on High for 1 minute and 15 seconds or until shiny. Stir in 1 cup almonds. Drop the dark chocolate and white chocolate in alternating dollops close together on a waxed paper-lined baking sheet. Swirl the chocolate together to marbleize with a knife held vertically; do not overmix.

Chill the mixture until firm and break into bite-size pieces. Store in the refrigerator or a cool place.

Serves 12   *Susan Behrens*

Holiday Peppermint Bark

24 hard peppermint candies
12 ounces (2 cups) white or dark chocolate chips
2 tablespoons shortening

Unwrap the peppermint candies and chop in a food processor or place them in a sealable plastic bag and crush into very small pieces with a rolling pin.

Combine the chocolate chips with the shortening in a medium microwave-safe dish. Microwave on High for 30 seconds and then stir. Repeat the process until the chocolate and shortening are melted and smooth. Shake the crushed candies into the chocolate through a colander, reserving the larger pieces in the colander.

Spread to the desired thickness on a waxed paper-lined baking sheet; press the reserved candy pieces gently onto the top. Chill or freeze until firm. Break into bite-size pieces. Store in an airtight container at room temperature or in the freezer for longer periods.

Makes 1 pound   *Kim Paterson*

Chocolate Truffles

2/3 cup heavy cream
12 ounces (2 cups) semisweet chocolate chips
2 teaspoons vanilla extract
1/4 cup unsweetened baking cocoa
3/4 cup sweetened shredded coconut, toasted
1/2 cup finely chopped unsalted pistachios

Bring the cream to a boil in a heavy medium saucepan and remove from the heat. Add the chocolate chips and whisk until the chocolate melts and the mixture is smooth. Whisk in the vanilla. Pour into a medium bowl and cover. Chill for 4 hours or until firm.

Drop the mixture by rounded teaspoonfuls onto a waxed paper-lined baking sheet. Freeze for 45 minutes or until firm.

Place the baking cocoa, coconut and pistachios in separate bowls. Roll the truffles in the hands until slightly warmed. Roll 1/3 of the truffles in the cocoa, 1/3 in the coconut and 1/3 in the pistachios. Return the truffles to the freezer if they become too soft during the process. Store the truffles, covered in plastic, in the refrigerator for up to 2 weeks.

Makes 2 1/2 dozen   *Deborah Titterton Narraway*

TRUFFLES

Truffles are a rich confection made with melted chocolate, butter or cream, sugar, and flavourings. Flavourings can include liquors, liqueurs, spices, vanilla, coffee, and/or nuts. After the mixture is cooled, it is shaped into balls. Coatings may include unsweetened cocoa, chocolate or candy sprinkles, coconut, coloured or shaved sugar, and chopped nuts. Truffles were so named because their irregular shape resembled the famous fungus.

Acknowledgements

SPONSORS

The Bank of Bermuda Ltd.

Marsh Management Services (Bermuda) Ltd.

Marsh Global Markets (Bermuda) Ltd.

Edmund Gibbons Ltd.

Transworld Oil Limited

PricewaterhouseCoopers

BF&M Insurance Group

The Bank of N.T. Butterfield & Son Ltd.

Cellular One Bermuda

Lindo's Market Ltd.

Lindo's Family Foods Ltd.

PHOTOGRAPHERS

Antoine AR Hunt

Antoine Hunt has been capturing the world on film for more than eleven years. He has travelled extensively, photographing landscapes around the world. He specialises in fine art photography, combining elements of the beginning of the 20th century's printing processes and concentrating on form and composition to develop his series Nature's Children. The concept behind the project is simply to photograph the world, not as separate places and territories but as one unified global ecosystem, recognising what we do not seem to appreciate—the life that gives us life!

His photographs have been displayed in exhibitions locally and internationally, including Bermuda, Mexico, and Greece. His clients have won numerous national and local design awards utilising his photography, and his images routinely appear in a variety of design publications island-wide.

Ann Spurling

Born in 1956 in Bermuda, Ms. Spurling was educated at St. George's Prep School and the Bermuda High School in Bermuda, Malvern Girls College in England, and graduated from the College of William and Mary in the U.S. with a Bachelor of Arts in English. She then attended the Doscher School of Photography for a year-long course in professional photography. Upon returning to Bermuda, Ms. Spurling worked for Mark Emmerson, a professional photographer, for one year before scaling the dizzy heights and plumbing the depths of self-employment in 1980.

Ms. Spurling and her husband Bruno Zupp have one son, Walker. In 1993, Ann and Bruno joined forces professionally to form Spurling and Zupp Studio. Ann's specialty is interior photography, but executive, food, editorial, and portrait photography are strong parts of her core business.

STOCK PHOTOGRAPHY

Roland Skinner

Amanda Temple

Bruno Zupp

Verdmont photograph courtesy of The Bermuda National Trust

Bermuda Rum Swizzle photograph courtesy of The Swizzle Inn

IMAGE COLOUR CORRECTION

Bermuda Homes and Gardens Publishing Company Limited

FLORAL ARRANGERS

Heather Brewer

Clotilde Daniel

Nola Haycock

Jan MacDonald

Elizabeth Parker

Susan Sickling

Cindy Young

FRIENDS AND MEMBERS OF THE BERMUDA JUNIOR SERVICE LEAGUE WHO PROVIDED ASSISTANCE

Government House

Lady Vereker

The Bermuda National Trust

Sir David and Lady Gibbons

Eric and Lorraine Hirschberg

Glenn and Susan Titterton

Reid and Linda Young

David and Louise Gibbons

Joe Gibbons

Danika Pereira

Jo Cook

Preston Hutchings

Richard and Cornelia Kempe

Roger and Mary Mello

Nikki Blagden

Kim Moseley

Lorri Lewis

Ginnie Cooper Stewart

Annette Cook

Paula Dilney Friend

Amy Stone

Lesley Page

Kathy Zuill

Joanne Ingham

Diana Chudleigh

Saltus Grammar School, SGY

Bermuda High School for Girls,
  IB Programme

Warwick Academy

Somerset Cricket Club

The International Sports Shop

Grand Central Deli

Thank you to the entire membership of The Bermuda Junior Service League for their support of this project, especially their assistance with our fundraising events and photo shoots.

Index

The Bermuda Junior Service League

serving the community since 1936

MISSION STATEMENT:

The Bermuda Junior Service League (BJSL) is an organisation of women committed to promoting volunteerism, developing the potential of women, and improving the community in which we live. Its purpose is educational and charitable.

HOW DID THE BERMUDA JUNIOR SERVICE LEAGUE BEGIN?

The BJSL has a long track record of making a positive difference in our community. The BJSL was founded by Mrs. C. Vail-Zuill in 1936, following the Junior League of America. During the early years, the League grew in a variety of activities that stemmed from its original concept of helping the King Edward VII Memorial Hospital (KEMH), the Welfare Society, and the Lady Cubbitt Compassion Association (LCCA). In 1953 the League was approached with regard to forming a hospital auxiliary to assist the KEMH, and, as a result, our Life Members formed the Women's Hospital Auxiliary (Pink Ladies), which today is an indispensable, separate organisation.

Today the BJSL continues to support a number of our original community projects along with a variety of new progressive projects as highlighted throughout the book. We are a diverse group of dedicated women who volunteer our time to make a difference in our community.

For additional copies of

Island Thyme

Please contact:

Bermuda market
The Bermuda Junior Service League
Web site: www.bjsl.bm
E-mail: IslandThyme@northrock.bm
Telephone: 441-292-4060

U.S. and International markets
FRP
www.cookbookmarketplace.com
Telephone: 800-269-6839

$37.95 plus shipping and handling